13+ English

For the Common Entrance exams

Preparing for the 13+ English exams is no small feat, but don't worry — CGP is here to explain everything you need to know to get you ready for the exams.

We've packed this brilliant book full of study notes, examples and plenty of practice questions — all bang up-to-date for the latest exams.

There are full answers at the back of the book, so you can easily keep track of your progress. So what are you waiting for, time to get stuck in!

How to access your free Online Edition

This book includes a free Online Edition to read on your PC, Mac or tablet.
You'll just need to go to **cgpbooks.co.uk/extras** and enter this code:

7374 6234 1860 3851

By the way, this code only works for one person. If somebody else has used this book before you, they might have already claimed the Online Edition.

Revision Guide

Contents

Section Six — Types of Writing

Section Seven — Using Language Effectively

Section Eight — Grammar

Section Nine — Punctuation

Section Ten — Spelling

Published by CGP

Editors:
Claire Boulter, Robbie Driscoll, Rebecca Greaves, Holly Poynton, Matt Topping and Adam Worster

With thanks to David Cageao and Tom Carney for the proofreading.

With thanks to Jan Greenway for the copyright research.

ISBN: 978 1 78908 795 6
Printed by Elanders Ltd, Newcastle upon Tyne.
Clipart from Corel®

Based on the classic CGP style created by Richard Parsons.

13+ English

Well, an introduction seems like a good place to start, so let's get cracking...

There are two **13+ English** exams

For 13+ English, there are two Common Entrance exams — a reading exam and a writing exam.

> If you're sitting 13+ exams set by your school, the exams might be structured differently to this. Ask your teacher what your exams will look like.

The **Reading** exam

- This exam lasts for 1 hour 10 minutes, which includes your reading and planning time.

- You will be given a text to read — it could be prose, poetry or drama.

- The exam is split into three sections that each contain questions about the text you've read.

- You should try to answer all of the questions. See p.2 for more information.

> There's also a Foundation version of the reading exam. In this exam, you will always be given a piece of prose — never poetry or drama.

The **Writing** exam

- This exam lasts for 1 hour 15 minutes, which includes your reading and planning time.

- It has one section with a choice of four questions.

- You should answer two of the questions.

- Each question will ask you to write a text from a choice of topics and styles. See p.42 for more information.

Spelling, Punctuation and Grammar are Important

1) The examiner will be looking at your spelling, punctuation, grammar and vocabulary in both exams.

2) In the exams you need to find a balance between working quickly and working carefully. You don't have much time, but you need to impress the examiner.

3) Luckily for you, this book has lots of handy information about spelling tricky words, punctuating sentences properly, using grammar correctly and how to use dazzling vocabulary.

Testing, testing, one two, one two...

This book is up and running and hopefully you're hearing me loud and clear. There's lots more coming up on both the reading exam and the writing exam, and how to be brilliant at both.

The Reading Exam

All your reading skills are assessed in the same exam, so make sure you know how it works.

The Reading paper has Three sections

For 13+ English, you'll take one of two reading papers — Paper 1 or the Foundation paper. Each paper has a Section A, a Section B and a Section C.

In Paper 1, you'll be given a passage of prose (fiction or non-fiction), a poem or an extract from a play. In Section A, you'll have to answer multiple-choice questions about the text. Section B will ask you some long-answer questions. In Section C, you'll write an essay about the text.

If you're sitting 13+ exams set by your school, the papers might be structured differently to this. Ask your teacher what your papers will look like.

Some tricky words in the text will be explained.

The Foundation paper contains a passage of prose. Section A asks multiple-choice questions about it. In Section B, there are some long-answer questions. Section C involves writing a creative response to the text.

You get 1 hour 10 minutes for the Reading Paper

1) Paper 1 and the Foundation paper both last for 1 hour 10 minutes.

2) Each paper is worth 50 marks — 15 marks for Section A, 25 marks for Section B and 10 marks for Section C.

3) That means you'll have roughly 20 minutes for Section A, 35 minutes for Section B and 15 minutes for Section C. Try to leave a couple of minutes at the end of each section to check your work for mistakes.

4) Work quickly but carefully — and always make sure you do what the question asks you.

Look at how many Marks you get for a Question

It's important to look at how many marks you get for each question so you know how long to spend answering each one.

Example

Which of the following best describes Harriet's new house?   [1]

You'll be given options for questions like this. This is only worth one mark, so don't spend ages on it. Come back to it later if you're not sure what the answer is.

Example

How does the author build tension in the third paragraph? Support your answer with evidence from the text.   [6]

This is worth six marks, so you'll need to give a bit more detail (see p.10-11).

Reading... I thought that was a place in Berkshire?

You're going to have to answer a few different types of questions in the exam, so it's a good idea to familiarise yourself with the reading paper you'll be taking so you'll know exactly what to do.

Novels

You might get an extract from a novel in the exam, so you need to know this stuff.

The **Perspective** is **Who** tells the story

Stories are normally written in the <u>first</u> or <u>third</u> person. A story that uses "<u>I</u>" or "<u>we</u>" is written in the <u>first</u> person. A story that uses "<u>he</u>", "<u>she</u>" or "<u>they</u>" is written in the <u>third</u> person.

I decided to join the circus.	She decided to join the circus.

This is in the <u>first person</u>. It makes the text seem more <u>personal</u> and <u>immediate</u>.

This is in the <u>third person</u>. It makes the text feel <u>less personal</u>.

The **Plot** is **What Happens**

The <u>plot</u> of a story is all the things that happen, in the <u>right order</u>.
A plot needs a <u>beginning</u>, a <u>middle</u> and an <u>end</u>.

Beginning

Jimmy has lost his dog.

Middle

Jimmy asks the neighbours if they've seen his dog. They haven't.

End

Jimmy finds the dog — it was sleeping under a pile of clothes.

The **Setting** is **Where** it **Happens**

Writers choose their settings <u>carefully</u>.
Where the story takes place is <u>important</u> for creating an <u>atmosphere</u>.

A horror story could be set in an old haunted house.	A science fiction story could be set in outer space.

The **Theme** is the **Deeper Meaning**

1) Themes include <u>love</u>, <u>greed</u>, <u>family</u>, <u>power</u> etc.

2) When you're writing about a novel, it's <u>not enough</u> to just identify the main theme — you need to make sure you comment on <u>how</u> the author <u>presents</u> the theme, or what they are <u>saying</u> about it.

Example

The theme of most fairy tales is good against evil. The good characters always win in the end. For example, Cinderella went to the ball and married the prince, and her ugly sisters got nothing.

A story that doesn't have a plot — a truly novel idea...

The terms on this page are nice and simple — make sure you know them. <u>Most stories</u> have a <u>perspective</u>, <u>plot</u>, <u>setting</u> and <u>theme</u>. Learn the page well so you know what to look out for.

Plays

Reading plays can get pretty confusing. But fear not! This page should make things simpler.

Plays are written to be Acted

1) There is a <u>massive difference</u> between a play and a novel or short story. A novel tells a story by <u>describing</u> it to you. A play tells a story by <u>showing</u> it to you.

2) You <u>don't</u> usually get any long describing bits in a play. The actors show the audience what's going on by the <u>way</u> they say their lines, as well as <u>what</u> they say.

3) The audience <u>doesn't</u> have the <u>play script</u> in front of them, so the <u>actors</u> have to do all the <u>work</u>.

When you read a play, you often have to work out what's going on just by reading the text and stage directions.

Stage Directions give a few clues

1) Stage directions show actors <u>what to do</u>, when to <u>come in</u> and when to <u>leave</u> the stage.

2) They're the words in <u>italics</u> and/or <u>brackets</u>, and they tell you the basics of what's <u>happening</u>.

3) <u>Always</u> read them when you read a play.

[*Enter Lady Hampton*]

"<u>Enter</u>" is a <u>stage direction</u>. It tells the person playing Lady Hampton to walk on stage.

[*Exeunt Lord Hampton and Archie*]

"<u>Exeunt</u>" is a daft word. All it means is that <u>more than one</u> person leaves the stage.

The Director decides the rest

1) Sometimes the stage directions <u>tell</u> the actors how to say their lines.

OMAR [*angrily*]   I cannot believe you broke another window!

"<u>angrily</u>" is a <u>stage direction</u>. It tells the actor playing Omar <u>how</u> to say this line.

2) More often, though, the <u>director</u> has to work out how the actors should say the lines — sadly, joyfully or whatever.

3) Unfortunately, you don't have a director in the test — you've got to figure it <u>all</u> out for yourself, from the <u>words</u>.

It might help if you try to imagine that you're the director. Ask yourself how you would direct the actors in the play you're reading.

REVISION TASK

His character is quiet — he reads between his lines...

Take a play you're studying or a film you've seen and think about one or two of its main characters. Jot down a couple of points about their appearance, what they say and what they do. Think about how these things make you <u>feel</u> about the character.

Travel Writing

Travel writing is like a diary written for someone else — it's really personal and very detailed.

Travel writing is full of Detailed Description

1) Travel writers work really hard to build up an image of the people and places they have seen.

2) There's always loads of detail and a big focus on setting.

> I looked at the road stretching before me like a shiny black ribbon. The air was intolerably close and a bead of sweat dropped from my forehead as I surveyed the dark, moody horizon.

Look out for descriptive and imaginative language. Think about how the writer is using their senses.

It's usually written in the First Person

1) Travel writing is often written from a first-person perspective, so the author will use 'I' a lot.

2) The writer is recording their own personal reaction to their surroundings, so they often talk about their thoughts and feelings.

3) The writer is trying to make you feel like you are there with them. But remember — everything is from their perspective — it's a bit like you're seeing it through their eyes.

Travel writers aren't shy — they're usually very quick to let you know how they feel about the people and places they are describing.

Travel writing can have Several Purposes

1) The main point of travel writing is to be entertaining. The writer wants to grab your attention with the exciting or amazing things they are describing.

2) They also want to give you information about the places they've been to.

3) So the purpose of the text is to entertain and inform.

Descriptive language informs the reader. → As the train chugged steadily through the beautiful, sloping valleys, I sat back and thought about how lucky I'd been. I took a deep breath and glanced up at the vibrant and charming woman I had just met. Then, to my horror, a monkey jumped out of her hat...

Humour is used to entertain the reader. →

Sometimes travel writing might try to persuade the reader to do something or go somewhere, but this depends on the text.

The forest burst to life with the cooing of wood pigeons...

A good travel writer can make their local wood seem like a rainforest. Okay, maybe not, but think about the techniques travel writers use to make their writing entertaining and informative for the reader.

Biographies and Autobiographies

Now for some more personal stuff. This time it's all about biographies and autobiographies...

Biographies and Autobiographies are Different

1) A biography is an account of someone's life story written by someone else.

2) An autobiography is an account of someone's life story written by that person.

3) Both biographies and autobiographies focus on the important moments in that person's life.

> At twenty-five, Ian became a father for the first time. → This is from a biography.

> The day I got married was the happiest day of my life. → This is from an autobiography.

Biographies are written in the Third Person

1) Biographies are written in the third person.

2) They're usually in the past tense as they're an account of events that have already happened.

3) Biographies usually only take into account the author's version of the events, so they're often biased (or one-sided).

Third person pronouns are used.

This is all written in the past tense.

> Stuart was elected as town mayor in July 1854. He was the best mayor that Newtron ever had and led the town's rugby team to a glorious victory over Protown in 1857. Stuart was replaced as mayor in 1862 after a controversial election.

Watch out for language that is subjective or biased.

Autobiographies are a bit like Diaries

1) Autobiographies are written in the first person and are extremely personal. They give lots of detail about the important moments in a person's life, and how the person felt about them.

2) The writer normally writes about events in chronological order, and explains how these experiences have moulded his or her personality.

3) They are often very touching, but they are written with the audience in mind — the writer is aiming to entertain and persuade the reader.

> January was a really tough month that year. Losing my job was a big blow, especially with all that Christmas debt that needed shifting. I was at an all-time low and began to make some really bad decisions...

This account is moving — you feel sympathy for the writer's situation.

The writer is trying to persuade you to look at things their way. They want to justify their choices and get you to believe their side of the story.

Don't just take my word for it...

...but if it's an autobiography, that's all you can do. Biographies and autobiographies tell you lots about someone, but remember — they're completely one-sided, so take them with a pinch of salt.

Poems

Petrified of poetry? Don't worry — this page will help you to start tackling poetry questions.

There are **Different Types** of **Poem**

Not all poems are the same. These are some <u>different kinds</u> of poem you might run into:

> <u>BALLADS</u> are poems that tell a <u>story</u>. They often have four-line verses and a <u>chorus</u>.

> <u>FREE VERSE</u> is a type of poem which <u>doesn't rhyme</u> and doesn't have a set line length.

> <u>SONNETS</u> are usually <u>14 lines</u> long, and have a special rhyme pattern.

A **Verse** is a **Section** of a poem

1) Poems are made up of <u>lines</u>.
2) <u>Lines</u> in a poem are often <u>repeated</u>.
3) A group of lines in a poem is called a <u>verse</u> — a verse is also known as a <u>stanza</u>.
4) Verses in a poem usually have <u>different</u> words, but they often follow the <u>same rhyme pattern</u>.

A **Poem** fits **A Lot** into a **Small Space**

In a poem, <u>how</u> things are said is just as important as <u>what</u> is said.
Here are a couple of verses from the poem 'The Brook' by Alfred Lord Tennyson.

<u>Figurative language</u> — e.g. <u>imagery</u> — is used to make the poem more interesting.

There's more on figurative language on p.18-19.

Think about why <u>particular words</u> have been chosen — each word needs to say a lot. E.g. Why has Tennyson chosen "eddying" here rather than "gushing" or "churning"?

> I chatter over stony ways,
> In little sharps and trebles,
> I bubble into eddying bays,
> I babble on the pebbles.
>
> [...]
>
> I slip, I slide, I gloom, I glance,
> Among my skimming swallows;
> I make the netted sunbeam dance
> Against my sandy shallows.

<u>Rhyme</u> and <u>rhythm</u> affect how the poem <u>sounds</u>. They put the focus on particular words. See <u>p.23-24</u> for more info.

REVISION TASK

One thing Tennyson's brook and I have in common?

We both like a good chatter. Find a copy of 'The Brook' by Alfred Lord Tennyson online, then choose a few words or phrases and explain why you think Tennyson used them.

Tackling Reading Questions

Now you know the types of text you might get asked about, it's time to deal with the questions...

READ THE QUESTIONS FIRST!

Skim-Read the text ~~First~~ *Again*

1) When you sit your reading exam, <u>read</u> the text you're given first, and then <u>read the questions</u>.

2) When you read the text, you should <u>skim-read</u>. Skim-reading gives a <u>rough idea</u> of what the writing is about. It's like looking at something <u>quickly</u> and having a <u>blurred</u> picture of it in your head. Look at it <u>carefully</u>, and you get more detail.

It's a bit like this. →

3) You can <u>jot down</u> any <u>key points</u> (like names or important events — see p.9), but don't spend long doing it.

Work Out what the questions are Asking

1) The questions will be about <u>the stuff you've just read</u>. You must read through each question very <u>carefully</u> before you even think about answering it.

2) Always remember the <u>magic question</u>. → **What is the question asking me to do?**

Example

Why is Lucia feeling irritated with her brother?   [2]

↖ This is asking you to write about why a <u>character feels</u> a certain way.

Example

How does the writer help you share Lucia's fear of heights?   [4]

↖ This is asking you to write about the <u>writer's choice of words</u>.

3) Whatever else you do, make sure your <u>answer</u> matches what the <u>question</u> is asking you to do. It's amazing how <u>easy</u> it is to slip up this way.

4) There's <u>no point</u> spending all your time in the first question talking about the writer's choice of words. Even if you do it <u>brilliantly</u>, it still won't be the right answer.

Questions — always looking for answers...

Skim-reading can <u>save you time</u> and help you get to grips with the text <u>quickly</u>. Hurray. Don't then go and waste all that good work by not answering the question you've been <u>asked</u>. Boo.

Finding the Important Bits

You have to agree — it's much easier to remember key points than a load of words.

Scan the writing for Key Words and Phrases

1) Once you've worked out what the question is asking you, you'll need to go back to the text and look for key words and phrases.

2) The key words and key phrases in a sentence or a paragraph will give you a really good idea of what it means. They're the things you'll need to answer the questions.

3) When you want to find those key bits of information, it's much quicker to let your eyes wander over the page on the lookout for the words you want. This is called scanning.

Find the bits that Answer the Question

Example

In what ways does the article make readers want to visit the castle?   [4]

1) The key to answering questions like this is to find loads of things in the article that help answer the question. This is where you need to scan for key words and phrases.

2) Here's the start of the article with the bits you need and the bits you don't need helpfully pointed out...

> Callendale Castle is built on a hill overlooking Callendale in West Bassetshire. On approaching Callendale village, the twin towers of the castle suddenly loomed through the mist, giving the village a mysterious appearance.
>
> Callendale Castle holds many stories, and many secrets. A quick read through the guidebook gave me a colourful insight into the way things must have been inside these forbidding stone walls all those years ago. A secret meeting between King Henry V and a French ambassador took place here during the Hundred Years War. In 1814, the castle narrowly escaped being burnt to the ground when a lazy kitchen boy left a pig roasting on the open fire unattended.
>
> The castle tour took me to a dark, dank dungeon, complete with gruesome instruments of torture. Hidden in one corner is a tiny cell, little more than a hole, where countless prisoners were left to rot away.

You don't need to say where the castle is.

Mention that it looks mysterious — that makes it sound interesting.

People would want to visit to find out more about the stories and secrets.

You don't need to retell these stories in your answer. Just say that the writer mentions them to maintain the reader's interest.

The writer spends some time talking about the dungeon. People find horrible things fascinating, so this bit is important.

3) There'll always be loads of stuff that's got nothing to do with the question. Don't write about every tiny little thing — only write about the bits that the question asks for.

I'm going to start collecting highlighters — mark my words...

It's a good idea to bring a highlighter into the exam with you. This means you can highlight key words and phrases when you first scan the text, making it easier to find them when you write your answer.

Writing Your Answer

Now you know how to pick out important bits from a text, it's time to learn how to write an answer.

Some questions ask you to Summarise Information

Some questions will ask you to summarise a piece of information in the text.
Have a look at this example question:

Example

Why does Katie enjoy travelling to new places?   [2]   ← This question is asking you to find some information in the text...

Katie enjoys learning about different cultures and meeting new people.   ← ...so all you need to do in the answer is summarise the information that the question is looking for to get your marks.

Some questions are a bit Trickier

Some questions want you to show whether you understand how certain effects are created in the text:

Example

How does the writer make you feel sympathy for Mr Hill?   [6]

This question is asking you to think about how the author has used language to make you feel sympathy for a character.

Use P.E.E. to write Answers to these questions

I'm not being silly. P.E.E. stands for: Point, Example, Explanation.
It's a great way to write an answer for these trickier types of question:

Point: Make a point that will answer the question.

Example: Give an example from the text.

Explanation: Show how the example backs up your point.

Start a new paragraph every time you make a new point.

Example

This is your example — a quotation from the text.

Use linking phrases like this when you start your next point.

The writer uses Mr Hill's past to make us feel sympathy for him. We're told that Mr Hill "always tried in vain" to please his father. This tells us that his father was never happy with anything he did.

Another person who treats Mr Hill badly is his supervisor at work. She is always telling him that...

This is your point.

This bit is your explanation.

In longer-answer questions, you'll also get marks for developing your points with analysis of the text's language and form.

First state the **Obvious**

1) You might read a question and think, "I can't think of anything <u>clever</u> to say." Don't worry — think of something <u>obvious</u> to say.

2) Sensible points will often be the right ones, even if they hardly seem worth saying at first.

3) If you notice something in the <u>text</u> that seems to answer the <u>question</u>, the chances are it <u>does</u>, so <u>write it down</u>.

4) <u>DON'T</u> think, "Oh, that's obvious, there's no point in putting that". Of course there's a point — the point is — <u>if it's right, write it down</u>.

Here's an example of making **Simple Points**

Look at this question and example answer:

Example

According to the text, how is Lee feeling as he waits for the dentist?   [3]

Lee shivered. He pulled his coat tightly around him, although it wasn't cold. His fists were clenched in his pockets. He stared at the floor in front of his feet and occasionally glanced nervously at the other people in the waiting room.

Here's your point.

Shivering and scared go together, so mention that he was shivering.

The writer shows that Lee was nervous and scared. Lee was shivering, "although it wasn't cold" which is often a sign that someone is nervous. The writer also suggests that Lee was...

Here's your example from the text that has something to do with the question.

And here's the explanation...

A new point, a new paragraph...

This answer may sound <u>simple</u>, but if you don't <u>write it down</u> then the examiner will think that you didn't notice it.

One way to think about it is to <u>pretend the examiner isn't very clever</u> — imagine that you have to <u>explain everything</u> to them using <u>simple points</u>.

Make sure that what you write is easy to understand.

No one will think you're stupid for stating the obvious...

So it's like this: make a <u>really simple point</u> that's <u>really obvious</u> in the text, back it up with a little <u>quotation</u> from the text itself, then <u>explain</u> how it <u>answers the question</u>. It's as easy as <u>P.E.E.</u>.

Warm-Up and Worked Practice Questions

Now that you've learned about the reading exam, try out these practice questions. If you're not sure about any of them, have a read back through the section to get some handy pointers.

Warm-Up Questions

1)   "He sprinted down the path, late for his bus again."
     Is this an example of first-person or third-person narration? How can you tell?

2)   The two main purposes of travel writing are:
     a) to describe and instruct.   b) to persuade and explain.
     c) to entertain and inform.   d) to argue and advise.

3)   Why might information in an autobiography be unreliable?

Worked Practice Question

Read the extract below from *The Importance of Being Earnest* by Oscar Wilde.
At this point in the play, Cecily and Gwendolen fall out,
as they believe they are both engaged to the same man.

CECILY	*[Rather shy and confidingly.]* Dearest Gwendolen, there is no reason why I should make a secret of it to you. Our little county newspaper is sure to chronicle the fact next week. Mr. Ernest Worthing and I are engaged to be married.
GWENDOLEN	*[Quite politely, rising.]* My darling Cecily, I think there must be some slight error. Mr. Ernest Worthing is engaged to me. The announcement will appear in the *Morning Post* on Saturday at the latest.
CECILY	*[Very politely, rising.]* I am afraid you must be under some misconception. Ernest proposed to me exactly ten minutes ago. *[Shows diary.]*
GWENDOLEN	*[Examines diary through her lorgnette* carefully.]* It is certainly very curious, for he asked me to be his wife yesterday afternoon at 5.30. If you would care to verify the incident, pray do so. *[Produces diary of her own.]* I never travel without my diary. One should always have something sensational to read in the train. I am so sorry, dear Cecily, if it is any disappointment to you, but I am afraid I have the prior claim.
CECILY	It would distress me more than I can tell you, dear Gwendolen, if it caused you any mental or physical anguish, but I feel bound to point out that since Ernest proposed to you he clearly has changed his mind. [...]

[Enter Merriman, followed by the footman. He carries a salver*, table cloth, and plate stand. Cecily is about to retort. The presence of the servants exercises a restraining influence, under which both girls chafe.]

The extract continues on the next page...

Worked Practice Questions

MERRIMAN	Shall I lay tea here as usual, Miss?
CECILY	*[Sternly, in a calm voice.]* Yes, as usual. *[Merriman begins to clear table and lay cloth. A long pause. Cecily and Gwendolen glare at each other.]*
CECILY	[...] May I offer you some tea, Miss Fairfax?
GWENDOLEN	*[With elaborate politeness.]* Thank you. *[Aside.]* Detestable girl! But I require tea!
CECILY	*[Sweetly.]* Sugar?
GWENDOLEN	*[Superciliously*.]* No, thank you. Sugar is not fashionable any more. *[Cecily looks angrily at her, takes up the tongs and puts four lumps of sugar into the cup.]*

* *lorgnette* — a magnifying glass   * *salver* — a tray   * *superciliously* — showing pride

1. How does the playwright present the relationship between Cecily and Gwendolen?

    Remember to use evidence from the extract in your answer.
    Explain what the evidence shows about Cecily and Gwendolen's relationship.

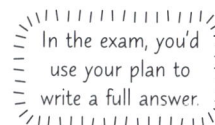

    In the exam, you'd use your plan to write a full answer.

PLAN

When writing an essay, always start by writing a plan. This is an example of how you could plan an answer to the question above.

INITIALLY HAVE A CLOSE BOND
*   Cecily speaks "confidingly" — suggests they are friends
*   refer to each other as "Dearest" and "darling"

UNDERLYING HOSTILITY MASKED BY POLITENESS
*   arguments phrased delicately — e.g. "there must be some slight error"
*   hints that they want to confront each other —
    e.g. Gwendolen "rising" followed by Cecily "rising"
*   "elaborate politeness" of Gwendolen's dialogue
    suggests her affection is now fake

Try to divide your answer up into logical parts.

BECOME MORE OPENLY HOSTILE
*   they "glare at each other" — suggests friendship is under strain
*   Cecily puts sugar in Gwendolen's tea at the end
    — does this deliberately to annoy her

CONCLUSION: friendly relationship becomes more hostile (hidden by polite dialogue),
until they become openly unfriendly towards each other (shown through stage directions)

Practice Questions

Practice Questions

This abridged extract is from *Persuasion*, a novel by Jane Austen. It was first published in 1817. Read the extract, then answer the questions that follow.

> Lady Dalrymple's carriage, for which Miss Elliot was growing very impatient, now drew up; the servant came in to announce it. It was beginning to rain again, and altogether there was a delay, and a bustle, and a talking, which must make all the little crowd in the shop understand that Lady Dalrymple was calling to convey* Miss Elliot. At last Miss Elliot and her friend, unattended but by the servant, [...] were walking off; and Captain Wentworth, watching them, turned again to Anne, and by manner, rather than words, was offering his services to her.
>
> "I am much obliged to you," was her answer, "but I am not going with them. The carriage would not accommodate so many. I walk: I prefer walking."
>
> "But it rains."
>
> "Oh! very little, Nothing that I regard."
>
> After a moment's pause he said: "Though I came only yesterday, I have equipped myself properly for Bath already, you see," (pointing to a new umbrella); "I wish you would make use of it, if you are determined to walk; [...]"
>
> She was very much obliged to him, but declined it all, repeating her conviction, that the rain would come to nothing at present, and adding, "I am only waiting for Mr Elliot. He will be here in a moment, I am sure."
>
> *convey* — accompany to a new place

1. Captain Wentworth offers Anne his help "by manner, rather than words".
   This means that he offers her help:
   a. unconsciously and out of habit.
   b. in a very polite way.
   c. through his body language.
   d. without being told to.

2. Which of the following statements is false?
   a. Anne doesn't mind walking in the rain.
   b. Captain Wentworth has recently arrived in Bath.
   c. Anne doesn't travel in the carriage because it is too full.
   d. It is raining heavily.

3. Which of the following words best describes Anne's behaviour towards Captain Wentworth?
   a. Hostile
   b. Polite
   c. Loyal
   d. Dishonest

Practice Questions

Use the extract on the previous page to answer the following questions.

4. What do you think Lady Dalrymple's social status is? Refer to the extract in your answer.

....

....

....

....

....

5. What is your impression of Anne? Use details from the extract in your answer.

....

....

....

....

....

....

6. How does the writer create a sense of busyness in the first paragraph?
    Support your answer with evidence from the extract.

....

....

....

....

....

....

Summary Questions

Wa-hey — made it to the end of the section. Time for some Summary Questions... Not the most exciting things ever, but these ARE extremely useful. You can test your knowledge on how to answer reading questions and make sure you know all the tricks and techniques of the trade. If there's anything you're stuck on, go straight back over those pages, and get it learned.

1) What is the difference between setting and perspective? ☐

2) Give two possible themes for a novel called "My Brother's Wedding". ☐

3) What is the point of stage directions in a play? ☐

4) How might imagining that you're a director help you when you're reading a play? ☐

5) Rewrite this sentence to turn it into a cracking sentence from a piece of travel writing: "They saw a tower in front of a forest and they could not believe it." ☐

6) What's the difference between a biography and an autobiography? ☐

7) Why might the writer of an autobiography use persuasive language? ☐

8) Name two different types of poem. ☐

9) What is a group of lines in a poem called? Give both possible answers. ☐

10) Why is it helpful to skim-read a text first, before you read it properly? ☐

11) A key word is:
   a) always the first word in a sentence,
   b) a word that is important in understanding the meaning of a text, or
   c) a word that gets you into locked places. ☐

12) How can 'scanning' help you to answer a question in your exam? ☐

13) How would your answers to these two questions differ?
   a) Find three words which describe the mongoose.
   b) How does the poet try to make the reader dislike the mongoose? ☐

14) What does P.E.E. stand for? (No funny business, mind.) ☐

15) Which of the statements below is true?
   a) You should pretend that your examiner is a genius and not make any simple points, or
   b) You should pretend that your examiner isn't very clever, and make simple points and explain things clearly. ☐

Choice of Vocabulary

Vocabulary is a just a fancy name for words. Writers have to choose their words carefully.

Think about the text's **Purpose** and **Audience**

Different texts will use different vocabulary depending on what
the purpose of the text is and who the audience is. For example:

> The vocabulary used by a character in a play reflects their personality. It could be formal or informal, depending on the impression the writer wants to give.

> A piece of travel writing will use lots of descriptive vocabulary.

> I never really connected with my uncle. We just didn't get on. He was a stubborn fellow and made it clear that he didn't like me...

Informal language is the kind of language you use with friends or family. A writer might use it to give a personal account, e.g. in an autobiography.

> The situation grew worse. By Monday, her position had become untenable.

Formal language is used for more serious stuff.
It's the type of language you might find in a classic novel.

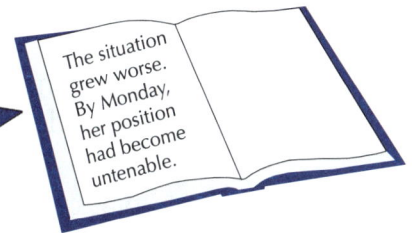

Slang makes a **Text** seem **Chatty**

1) Slang is really informal language.

Informal language is sometimes called 'colloquial language'.

2) Characters in novels or plays often use slang in their dialogue (when they're talking), as it makes speech sound more natural.

3) Some informal texts use slang to make the readers feel that the narrator is chatting to them. Here are some examples of slang:

> I needed some grub.

> "Cheers, mate!"

> We spotted the celebs in Coventry.

Technical Language makes a text seem **Informative**

1) Technical language uses lots of specialist words that are specific to a certain topic. It shows that the writer knows a lot about that subject.

> Average worldwide temperatures have increased by about 1°C in the last hundred years, mainly due to increased emission of gases such as carbon dioxide.

2) Sometimes a character or narrator will use technical language to make what they're saying seem more persuasive.

This is an example of technical language. It uses specialist terms like 'emission' and 'carbon dioxide'.

Use yer crust — learn this blinder of a page...

When you're reading, bear in mind that writers are very picky when choosing the words for their texts. Ask yourself why they chose the words they did and what effect they wanted to achieve.

Figurative Language

Figurative language can have a very powerful effect on the reader. Read on to see how...

Figurative Language makes texts more Interesting

Figurative language makes a text more appealing and engaging.
Examples of figurative language include:

imagery   onomatopoeia   personification   exaggeration

similes   alliteration   metaphors

A Simile says something is Like something else

A simile is a way of describing something by saying it's like something else.
Similes usually use the words "as", "like" or "than".

The thief crept up as quietly as a mouse.

This is a simile. It tells you how quiet the thief was.

I'd forgotten my gloves and soon my fingers were like blocks of ice.

This is a simile. It tells you how cold his fingers were.

A Metaphor says something Is something else

Metaphors describe something by saying that it is something else.
They never use 'like' or 'as'. For example:

Julius is a pig when he eats.

This is a metaphor. Julius isn't actually a pig, but the writer is suggesting that Julius is like a pig because he eats so greedily.

Imagery is about making a Picture

Imagery uses words to create a picture in the reader's mind.
Writers often use similes and metaphors to do this.

The desert stretched out before us, as white and as empty as the surface of the moon.

The strawberries were fragrant jewels, freshly picked and glistening.

Personification is another kind of Comparison

Personification is when something is described as if it's a person.

| The autumn leaves danced playfully in the wind. | The sun smiled on the people below. |

Leaves can't actually dance, but it creates an interesting image for the reader.

The personification makes it sounds like the sun has a human expression and sets an upbeat tone.

Writers Exaggerate for Effect

Exaggeration is when an unrealistic comparison is made for effect. It's also called hyperbole.

| Jack was as tall as a tree. | Freda was as old as the hills. |

Trees are pretty tall, and hills are pretty old, so these are good comparisons. You don't literally mean that Jack was as tall as a tree or Freda was as old as a hill — but people will understand.

Alliteration is when Sounds are Repeated

When lots of words start with the same sound, it's called alliteration.

The acclaimed actors flocked to the famous film festival.

This sentence has two lots of alliteration.

When words contain the same vowel sound, it's called assonance.

Even though they're spelt differently, these vowel sounds are the same, so it's assonance.

The game changed when we had the weight of eight men behind us.

Onomatopoeia — Sounds Like what it's talking about

Some words sound a bit like the noise they're talking about — this technique is called onomatopoeia. Writers use onomatopoeia to make their descriptions sound more effective.

"Crunch" went Pedro's bike, as he smashed into the car.

The car screeched to a halt.

This page is more helpful than a life jacket in a flood...

Maybe that's an exaggeration. But it's still pretty useful. If you want to sound like you know your stuff when you're writing about a text, learning these terms will be dead handy. Trust me.

Mood

This isn't about someone having a sulk in the corner — it's about how a text makes you feel.

The **Mood** of a **Text** is how it makes you **Feel**

1) The writer uses language to create the mood in a piece of text.

2) A text can make us feel happy, sad or even scared... Boo!

Look for **Devices** that **Create** the **Mood**

1) When you read a text, look for words that make you feel a certain emotion. That will help you to work out the mood of the text.

   For example, the writer's language can create a positive or happy mood in the text.

Words like 'jubilant' and 'triumphantly' create a happy mood.

> Feeling jubilant, Kay let himself freewheel down the hill, the wind blowing triumphantly through his hair. The birds whistled in the trees, cheering him on. He grinned. He was going to win now, without a doubt.

This is personification. It's used here to show how positive Kay feels.

2) Writers also use some clever techniques to build the mood. For example, short words and short, sharp sentences can create an atmosphere of tension.

Words like 'suddenly' create a sense of shock.

Metaphors can create images that add to the sense of fear.

> Suddenly, the floorboard creaked. Prakash froze. His heart pounded in his chest. His blood turned to ice. He was going to be caught. He knew it.

Short sentences add tension.

3) Another technique is using ellipses to create suspense:

> Holding her breath, Lucy reached with trembling hands to stack the last two cards on the tower... If it fell now, all her hard work would be ruined...

Ellipses create a pause, which can add suspense.

4) Nothing in a text is accidental. A writer chooses their words deliberately to make the readers feel happy, or sad, or tense, or excited, or whatever.

REVISION TIP

Nothing can make my bad mood bett– Ooh, puppies!

First learn the techniques that writers use to create moods. Then try spotting them in the texts you read. It gets easier with practice, so get reading and you'll be great at it in no time.

Characterisation

You need to learn how writers show their characters' personalities in their texts.

Writers tell you about their Characters

1) The way a writer gives the reader information about their characters is called characterisation.

2) You can learn about characters by what they say and do, what other characters say about them, and from their own thoughts and feelings (especially if the text is written in the first person).

"I'll show you around," Hajira said kindly. "I remember how scary it is being the new kid."

From what she says, we can see that Hajira's character is kind and helpful.

The sorcerer cackled slyly to himself. He was going to make them pay...

The sorcerer's actions ("cackled slyly") show us that he is cruel. He's also thinking about revenge.

"Whatever you do, don't upset the chef," Paul warned. "He's got a short temper and a sharp tongue."

Here, another character describes the chef, so the reader finds out that he gets cross easily.

There are Different Types of Character

In stories and plays there are different types of character.
There can be evil characters, good characters, funny characters, etc...

Sometimes these different types of character can stand for certain ideas.
For example, a character could represent love, evil or authority.

A teacher could be used to represent wisdom.

A greedy businessman could represent corruption.

If I were a character, I would represent perfection...

Of course, some characters are not straightforward good or evil types. They can be a bit more complicated than that. But you should be able to spot the simple ones when they do crop up.

Irony and Symbolism

Sometimes you have to read between the lines of a text to discover its real meaning...

Irony can add Humour to texts

1) Irony is when someone says one thing but means another.
   It can be used to entertain a reader by making the text funnier.

   > What a great idea of mine to go for a nice long walk on the rainiest day of the year.

   It's clear the narrator doesn't think it was a great idea to go for a walk on a particularly rainy day — they are being ironic.

2) Something is ironic if there's a big difference between what people expect and what actually happens.

   > Dr Martinez ran across the road to avoid getting wet in the rain, but he tripped and fell into a puddle right up to his chin.

   This is ironic because Dr Martinez thought he'd get less wet by running across the road — actually, he got more wet.

3) Irony is often used to make texts more interesting and add layers of meaning.

   > Water, water, everywhere,
   > Nor any drop to drink.

   In his poem, 'The Rime of the Ancient Mariner', Coleridge describes the irony of a stranded ship surrounded by sea water, but without a drop of water that the crew can drink.

Symbols give things a more Significant Meaning

1) You'll come across symbols in everyday life, e.g. a yawn symbolises someone being bored.

2) Symbolism is when objects or actions are used to signify ideas beyond what is obvious.

3) Traditional examples in literature include a dove symbolising peace, or a red rose symbolising love.

   > My heart leaps up when I behold
   > A rainbow in the sky:

   In this poem, William Wordsworth uses the rainbow as a symbol of hope.

A literary cymbal? Sounds noisy and annoying...

REVISION TASK

Get to grips with irony and symbolism by learning the effects of each technique.
When you think you're ready, have a go at writing a few of your own examples.

Poetry Conventions

Rhyming is pretty darn important in poems. Time to see how it all works...

Words **Rhyme** if their **Endings** sound the **Same**

Although poems <u>don't</u> have to rhyme, rhyme is used <u>a lot</u> so you need to <u>understand</u> how it works. Rhyming words are words that <u>sound</u> the same.

Little Bo Peep has lost her sheep.

"Peep" and "sheep" rhyme. They have the same "<u>-eep</u>" ending.

down   clown   frown   town

These words rhyme. They have the same "<u>-own</u>" ending.

late   eight   mate   plate   straight

The endings don't have to be spelt the same way. They just have to <u>sound</u> the same.

A **Rhyming Couplet** is **Two Consecutive Lines** that rhyme

If a line of poetry rhymes with the next one, you've got a rhyming couplet. Lots of poetry is made of rhyming couplets.

This is an extract from the poem 'The Land of Story-books' by Robert Louis Stevenson:

At evening when the lamp is lit,
Around the fire my parents sit;
They sit at home, and talk and sing,
And do not play at anything.

Lit rhymes with sit.

Sing rhymes with thing.

Here's another example from a nursery rhyme:

Ring a ring of roses
A pocket full of posies.

Roses rhymes with posies. (It isn't such an exact rhyme this time.)

Repetition emphasises **Key Ideas**

Poets <u>repeat</u> words, <u>phrases</u>, and even <u>whole lines</u>, in order to <u>emphasise</u> points in their poems. If you spot a word or phrase that's <u>repeated</u>, you can be sure that it's <u>important</u>...

These lines are from Robert Burns's poem, 'My Heart's in the Highlands'.

The word "<u>heart</u>" is repeated three times in two lines. This suggests that the poet feels very <u>emotional</u>.

My heart's in the Highlands, my heart is not here;
My heart's in the Highlands a-chasing the deer;

The poet repeats "<u>the Highlands</u>" — he is clearly <u>thinking</u> about this place <u>a lot</u>.

Rhythm is important in Poetry

A lot of poetry follows a rhythm pattern. There might be a fixed pattern of syllables on each line. If a line has too many syllables, it won't fit with the rest of the verse.

> Jack and Jill went up the hill,
> To fetch a pail of water.
> Jack fell down and broke his crown,
> While Jill stood at the top laughing at him for being so clumsy.

There are far too many syllables here...

A syllable is a part of a word that can be said in a single sound, e.g. 'family' has three syllables — 'fam-i-ly'.

Metre means the Rhythm of a poem

Metre is the name for the rhythm and syllable pattern of a poem.

A syllable is stressed if you emphasise it more, e.g. mag-a-ZINE, vol-CA-no, CU-cum-ber.

Some poetry has a pattern of stressed and unstressed syllables that mirrors normal speech. It gives poetry a very natural rhythm.

> My mistress' eyes are nothing like the sun.

Sometimes this rhythm is disrupted to emphasise a particular word. Look at how Alexander Pope uses a disrupted rhythm to change the emphasis in this quotation.

> To err is human; to forgive, divine.

Two unstressed syllables together disrupts the flow of the line — it puts the focus on 'forgive'. Ending on a stressed syllable gives the line a sense of authority and certainty.

You need to Think about the poem's Structure

A poem's structure is made up of its lines, verses, rhyme pattern and rhythm. Some poems, like sonnets, have a set structure, e.g. most sonnets have 14 lines. Have a look at the structure of 'The Eagle' by Alfred Lord Tennyson.

> He clasps the crag with crooked hands;
> Close to the sun in lonely lands,
> Ringed with the azure world, he stands.
>
> The wrinkled sea beneath him crawls;
> He watches from his mountain walls,
> And like a thunderbolt he falls.

This poem has two verses and each verse has three lines.

Each line has eight syllables.

Every line in each verse rhymes.

Read carefully, and you'll notice that every other syllable is stressed.

Metre — not just one hundred centimetres...

Rhythm and metre are trickier than rhyme so re-read this page till they're both clear in your mind. Then cover the page and jot it all down from memory — you'll be a poetry whizz in no time.

Warm-Up and Worked Practice Questions

Buckle up, folks — it's question time. Ease yourself in by trying out these warm-up questions.

Warm-Up Questions

1) Name five types of figurative language.

2) Which of the following are examples of hyperbole?
   a) Margo is as fast as a cheetah.
   b) The seagull swooped over the sea.
   c) The meat sizzled as it cooked.
   d) The bag was as heavy as a boulder.

3) Picture this scene: "Charlie opened the present with a sneer."
   What does the word "sneer" tell us about Charlie's reaction to the present?

4) What is symbolism?

5) Why might a poet disrupt the rhythm of their poem?

Read on for an example of how you could answer an exam-style question.

Worked Practice Question

Read this extract from the novel *Hard Times* by Charles Dickens.
In the extract, Dickens describes a character called Mr Bounderby.

He was a rich man: banker, merchant, manufacturer, and what not. A big, loud man, with a stare, and a metallic laugh. A man made out of a coarse material, which seemed to have been stretched to make so much of him. A man with a great puffed head and forehead, swelled veins in his temples, and such a strained skin to his face that it seemed to hold his eyes open, and lift his eyebrows up. A man with a pervading appearance on him of being inflated like a balloon, and ready to start. A man who could never sufficiently vaunt* himself a self-made man. A man who was always proclaiming, through that brassy speaking-trumpet of a voice of his, his old ignorance and his old poverty. A man who was the Bully of humility*.

A year or two younger than his eminently* practical friend, Mr. Bounderby looked older; his seven or eight and forty might have had the seven or eight added to it again, without surprising anybody. He had not much hair. One might have fancied he had talked it off; and that what was left, all standing up in disorder, was in that condition from being constantly blown about by his windy boastfulness.

* *vaunt* — boast, brag   * *humility* — modesty   * *eminently* — exceptionally

1. What impression of Mr Bounderby does the writer create in this passage?
   Remember to refer to the text in your answer.

> Dickens creates the impression that Mr Bounderby is an unpleasant and
>
> unlikable man. Dickens does this by using various language techniques to affect
>
> the reader's perception of the character. For example, Mr Bounderby is described
>
> as being "loud" and he has a voice like a "speaking-trumpet". Comparing

The answer continues on the next page...

Worked Practice Questions

Mr Bounderby's voice to a trumpet is effective because it is a recognisable

sound to the reader, and it emphasises the loudness and brashness of his voice.

Additionally, since trumpets are used for fanfares, this reinforces the idea that

Mr Bounderby is a boastful character who is a "Bully of humility". ← *Embedding your quotes will impress the examiner.*

    Dickens also uses the simile "inflated like a balloon" to make

Mr Bounderby's appearance seem ridiculous. This image of him being inflated

is echoed earlier in the passage when he is described as having a "puffed head"

and "swelled veins". Together, these descriptions present a grotesque image of

Mr Bounderby, and create the sense that he is overflowing with self-importance.

    Furthermore, while Dickens uses language to make Mr Bounderby seem

unpleasant, he also encourages the reader to ridicule Mr Bounderby. For example,

he suggests that Mr Bounderby has "talked" his hair off. Ridiculous images such

as these cause the reader to see Mr Bounderby as a comical character. ← *Keep referring back to the effect on the reader.*

The last worked practice question was for a fiction text — now get ready for a non-fiction one.

Worked Practice Question

Read the review of a theme park below, then answer the question on the following page.

Why on earth would anyone want to visit a theme park? That's the question I asked myself after taking my kids to one last weekend.

I started to have niggling doubts from the moment we arrived. First of all, we got there an hour after the park had opened, but we still had to sit in a queue of traffic before we could even park the car. Unfortunately, this was a sign of things to come.

Once we were wedged into a parking space the size of a postage stamp, we followed the herd to the entrance gates, a mere 25-minute walk away — not ideal when your kids are already squirming with impatience.

Then, we joined another queue to hand over our hard-earned money to the spotty youth in the ticket kiosk. For a family of four, it cost over 100 quid. My eyes watered as I relinquished the cash.

After what felt like a lifetime, we made it into the park. A luminous information board told us that one of the rides was shut due to strong winds, another was closed due to compulsory maintenance and the rest had queue times of about 80 minutes. By this point, I didn't think the day could get any better.

Worked Practice Questions

1. How does the writer convey their attitude to the theme park in this extract?

You should write three paragraphs, each focusing on a different point.
Remember to give evidence from the text throughout your answer.
Explain how the evidence you've chosen conveys the writer's attitude.

The writer of the text clearly has a very negative attitude towards the theme park. They convey this attitude through their narrative style, their use of figurative language and their sarcastic tone.

The introduction is simple but clear.

Make sure the focus of each paragraph is clear.

Firstly, the writer conveys their attitude through their narrative style. The text is written in the first person: for example, the writer says "I started to have niggling doubts". By using first-person narration, the writer creates the impression that they are talking directly to the reader, which makes their negative experience at the theme park seem more believable and relatable. The writer also tries to connect with the reader by using informal language. The use of slang ("kids", "cash", "quid") and contractions ("That's", "didn't") creates a chatty voice, which makes it sound as though the writer is talking to the reader like a friend. By doing this, the writer encourages the reader to relate to them, which helps the reader to feel sympathy for the writer's negative experience.

Remember to use linking words.

Secondly, the writer uses figurative language to convey their negative attitude towards the theme park. For example, they say that their car parking space was "the size of a postage stamp" and that it took "a lifetime" to make it into the park. These examples of hyperbole emphasise the writer's frustration about the facilities at the theme park. The writer also uses imagery to explain why their experience was negative. For example, they compare the crowd to a "herd", which emphasises how busy the park was.

Use plenty of quotes.

The answer continues on the next page...

Practice Questions

Thirdly, throughout the text, the writer uses a sarcastic tone. They say that it was a "mere 25-minute walk" to the entrance and that they "didn't think the day could get any better" when they encountered problems in the park. This use of sarcasm creates humour, as it feels like the writer is sharing a joke with the reader.

Talk about the effect of language.

This also makes the reader sympathise with the writer and their negative experience.

In conclusion, the writer uses a number of techniques to convey their attitude towards the park. Most of these techniques are used to encourage the reader to feel sympathy for the writer, which would make the reader more likely to agree with the writer's negative attitude towards the theme park.

The conclusion summarises how the writer conveys their attitude.

Now it's your turn. Practise what you've learned by having a go at answering these questions.

Practice Questions

In this extract from a poem, the poet is watching as it snows.
Read the extract, then answer the questions on the following page.

An extract from 'The Snow Fairy' *by Claude McKay*

Throughout the afternoon I watched them there,
Snow-fairies falling, falling from the sky,
Whirling fantastic in the misty air,
Contending fierce for space supremacy.
And they flew down a mightier force at night,
As though in heaven there was revolt and riot,
And they, frail things had taken panic flight
Down to the calm earth seeking peace and quiet.
I went to bed and rose at early dawn
To see them huddled together in a heap,
Each merged into the other upon the lawn,
Worn out by the sharp struggle, fast asleep.
The sun shone brightly on them half the day,
By night they stealthily had stol'n away.

Practice Questions

1. Look at the first 8 lines. Which of the statements below is true?
   a. It stops snowing during the night.
   b. It snows more heavily during the night.
   c. It begins snowing during the night.
   d. It snows less heavily during the night.

2. The poem says that, by the end of the second day, the snow-fairies
   "stealthily had stol'n away". This means that:
   a. more snow had fallen.
   b. the snow had melted.
   c. the snow-fairies had taken the heat away.
   d. the snow-fairies had stopped huddling together.

3. a) Find two quotes that describe the snow-fairies.
   b) Explain what each quote suggests about the snow-fairies.

   ....
   ....
   ....
   ....
   ....
   ....
   ....

4. How does the poet create an atmosphere of magic and wonder in the poem?

   ....
   ....
   ....
   ....
   ....
   ....
   ....

Practice Questions

Practice Questions

Read this description of a beach and answer the questions below.

> The tide was out; the beach was deserted; lazily flopped the warm sea. The sun beat down, beat down hot and fiery on the fine sand, baking the grey and blue and black and white-veined pebbles. It sucked up the little drop of water that lay in the hollow of the curved shells; it bleached the pink convolvulus* that threaded through and through the sand-hills. Nothing seemed to move but the small sand-hoppers. Pit-pit-pit! They were never still.
>
> Over there on the weed-hung rocks that looked at low tide like shaggy beasts come down to the water to drink, the sunlight seemed to spin like a silver coin dropped into each of the small rock pools. They danced, they quivered, and minute ripples laved* the porous shores. And how strong, how damp the seaweed smelt in the hot sun...
>
> The green blinds were drawn in the bungalows of the summer colony. Over the verandas, prone on the paddock, flung over the fences, there were exhausted-looking bathing-dresses and rough striped towels. Each back window seemed to have a pair of sand-shoes on the sill and some lumps of rock or a bucket or a collection of pawa* shells. The bush quivered in a haze of heat; the sandy road was empty except for the Trouts' dog Snooker, who lay stretched in the very middle of it. His blue eye was turned up, his legs stuck out stiffly, and he gave an occasional desperate-sounding puff, as much as to say he had decided to make an end of it and was only waiting for some kind cart to come along.

convolvulus — a type of flower   *laved* — washed   *pawa* — a type of pearly shell

Extract from *At the Bay* by Katherine Mansfield

1. Look at the first paragraph. How does the writer present the weather on the beach? Support your answer with references to the text.

....

....

....

....

....

....

....

2. Look at the whole text. How does the writer create a relaxed mood?

Remember to give evidence from the text throughout your answer.
Explain how the evidence you've chosen creates a relaxed mood.
Write your answer on a separate piece of paper.

Summary Questions

Finished these pages on reading? Feeling ready to go? Then go ahead and run through these questions. If any of them fox you, go back through this section until you find the answer.

1) An actor is playing a scientist in a play. He is explaining astrophysics.
   His lines will mostly use:
   a) simple, easy language   b) technical language   c) slang

2) Decide whether the following sentences are similes or metaphors:
   a) The palms of her hands were sandpaper.
   b) He was a beast with the ball.
   c) The car was like an oven.
   d) The snow lay over the fields like a white blanket.

3) What is personification?

4) Which words in these sentences are examples of onomatopoeia?
   a) The snake hissed unhappily as they looked at it through the glass.
   b) They uncorked the bottle of champagne with a loud pop.
   c) The collection of tins clanged and clattered in the boot of the car.

5) What is the effect of using short words or short, sharp sentences in a text?
   a) It makes everyone laugh until their sides ache.
   b) It makes it seem more soppy and romantic.
   c) It helps create a feeling of tension.

6) Why do writers use ellipses?

7) The way a writer gives the reader information about their characters is called personalisation. True or false?

8) Which of these things help us to learn about characters?
   a) The things they say
   b) Their thoughts and feelings
   c) Their star signs
   d) Their baking abilities
   e) The things other characters say about them

9) What is irony?

10) Name something that could be used as a symbol of evil in a literary text.

11) Pair up the rhyming words:
    mane   gate   mine   plain   tea   see   straight   fine

12) A rhyming couplet is only made up of two lines. True or false?

13) Why might a poet repeat a word in a line or verse?

14) What is the difference between a stressed and an unstressed syllable?

15) Lara McLaughalot says, "A metre is a hundred centimetres.
    It's nothing to do with poetry." Explain why she is wrong.

Give Reasons

Anything you write / think about

In this section, you'll be trained to give reasons for anything and everything...

Always give examples from the text.

Give Reasons from the Text

1) You have to give <u>reasons</u> for what you say by using <u>examples</u> from the passage you've read.

2) They show <u>where</u> your answer has <u>come from</u>.

3) If you <u>don't</u> give reasons, your answer won't show <u>you know</u> what you're talking about.

4) <u>Examples</u> show you haven't got it right by <u>lucky fluke</u>. Here's a handy example...

Example

The women at the book club aren't very friendly. In fact they're very rude.

This answer <u>doesn't</u> give any reasons...

Example

The women at the book club are not very welcoming: they ignore Mrs Irvine when she tries to say hello. They even look at her and then start talking among themselves. This makes them seem very rude.

...but this answer gives a <u>reason</u> from the writing to justify every point it makes. That's loads better.

Every Time you make a Point — give an Example

1) It's easy to <u>forget</u> to give examples from the bit of writing you've read. But your answer will make <u>more sense</u> and have a <u>clearer structure</u> if you give <u>proof for every point</u> you make.

2) It's best to <u>imagine</u> that the person reading your answers has <u>never seen the text</u> you're talking about.

3) Drum this <u>simple rule</u> into your head:

<u>Every time</u> you make a <u>point</u>, <u>back it up</u> with an <u>example</u>.

Give reasons — and currants, and sultanas...

The <u>sure-fire</u> way to write really good responses and to prove your inner English genius is to cram loads of <u>examples</u> into your answer. <u>Reasons</u> and <u>examples</u> — keep 'em coming.

Using Your Own Words

When you link your answer to the text you've read, use new words to show you understand it.

Don't just Copy bits out

When you give your answer, don't just copy out what the text says, word for word.
Anyone can do that, so it doesn't prove that you've understood it.

Here's part of a story:

> Mrs Irvine began to introduce herself. But the sour-faced woman turned away and started to talk to her companions.

And here's a possible answer about it...

Example

When Mrs Irvine began to introduce herself, the sour-faced woman turned away and started to talk to her companions.

This isn't a good way to talk about the story. It uses all the same words as the story — it doesn't show that you actually understand it.

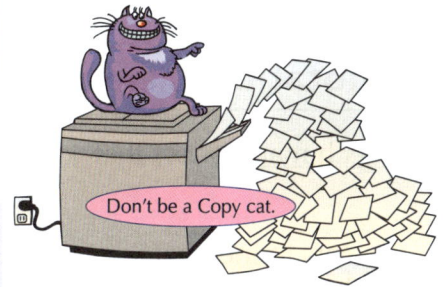

Don't be a Copy cat.

Put the reason in Your Own Words instead

Prove you've understood what you've read — use your own words.
Here is a much better answer about the bit of text above.

Example

The woman ignored Mrs Irvine when she tried to introduce herself.

This answer paraphrases the text above — it uses different words to say the same thing.

Remember — when you're giving a reason, always use your own words.

Tracing teeth marks? — Don't copy 'bites' out...

You know you have to give reasons and explanations in your answers and that means you've got to use your own words. So kick-start your brain and say it your way — don't just copy it.

How to Quote

Your answer won't be complete if you don't stick in loads of lovely quotations...

Quote, Quote, Quote — and Quote some More

1) It's not a good idea to copy out what a piece says word for word, but quoting is a great way to improve your answer.

2) Quotations are great because they show exactly which bit you've got your answer from.

3) Quoting isn't the same as stealing words from the text you've read. There's a massive difference.

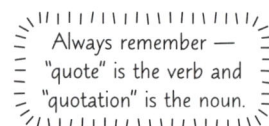

> Always remember —
> "quote" is the verb and
> "quotation" is the noun.

Quotations have Speech Marks

Speech marks show that you're quoting, not stealing words. Here's an example:

> Mrs Irvine began to introduce herself. But the sour-faced woman turned away and began to talk to her companions. All the other women glanced briefly at Mrs Irvine.

Example

The writer describes one woman as "sour-faced". That makes us think she's not a nice person.

Everything inside the speech marks is a quotation. It has to be what the text says word for word.

Be careful you don't get confused between these two:

Backing up a point with a reason — use your own words.
Backing up a point with a quotation — copy that bit of text exactly and put it in speech marks.

Some quotations are a Bit Tricky

1) If you're quoting more than one line of poetry, put a '/' to show where a new line starts:

Example

William Wordsworth, in his poem 'Daffodils', describes his happiness when he thinks about daffodils: "my heart with pleasure fills, / And dances with the daffodils".

2) If you're quoting from a play, you must make it clear who's speaking:

Example

On line 7, Camila claims that "Humphrey is as useful as an inflatable pincushion".

Quote early, quote often...

Everyone will love you if you quote bits from the text*. Remember — copying is bad, quoting is good. Oh, and don't forget, quotations always have to have speech marks.

*Although I can't prove that point.

Explain the Quotation

You always have to make sure you explain why you're using a quotation.

Put the explanation **Before** the quotation

Here, a quotation is used to <u>back up a reason</u> that's been given:

The answer <u>makes a point</u> — it says the women are rude.

Then there's <u>a reason to back it up</u> — the women talk among themselves even though they know Mrs Irvine is there.

Example

The women at the book club are rude. They talk amongst themselves even though they all know Mrs Irvine is there — "All the other women glanced briefly at Mrs Irvine".

Now there's a quotation from the text. The quotation <u>proves the point</u> that the other women all know Mrs Irvine is there.

Or give the quotation **First**

Here a quotation is used <u>first</u>, and followed by an <u>explanation</u>.

Always explain why the quotation is relevant.

Example

The writer describes one woman as "sour-faced". That makes us think she's not a nice person.

This time the quotation gets in there <u>first</u>. Then the answer explains why it's <u>relevant</u> to the point — that she isn't nice.

If you just wrote this bit, your answer <u>wouldn't</u> be entirely <u>complete</u> — you're not really making a point. You need to explain <u>why</u> you think the quotation is important or what its <u>effect</u> is in the text.

The writer describes one woman as "sour-faced".

It <u>doesn't matter</u> what order you do it in — make a point, then back it up with a quotation — or quote then explain. The important thing is that you <u>always explain why</u> your quotation <u>helps</u> your <u>point</u>.

The safari quotation was nice but irrelephant...

REVISION TIP

<u>You'll know</u> why you've chosen a quotation, but the examiner won't — you'll need to <u>tell them</u> why it's been used. As you revise, practise explaining <u>why</u> you've chosen quotations.

Keeping Quotations Short

Keep your quotations short and sweet — mega-long quotations can confuse readers...

Never quote more than a Few Words...

Quotations show that you've read and understood the text you're talking about. You usually only need to quote a few words. Look at this example from 'Porphyria's Lover' by Robert Browning.

Example

Browning creates a tense atmosphere by describing a brutal storm with human characteristics:
"The rain set early in tonight,
The sullen wind was soon awake,
It tore the elm-tops down for spite,
And did its worst to vex the lake:
I listened with heart fit to break."

This quotation is far too long. If your quotations are muddled, you'll sound unsure. Extra-long quotations could also confuse your reader.

Example

Browning creates a tense atmosphere by describing a brutal storm with human characteristics: "The sullen wind was soon awake".

This quotation is loads better. It's short and it has everything you need to make your point.

Here's another example from Rupert Brooke's poem, 'The Soldier':

Example

The poet tries to find comfort in the idea of dying at war:
"And think, this heart, all evil shed away,
A pulse in the eternal mind, no less
Gives somewhere back the thoughts by England given;
Her sights and sounds; dreams happy as her day;
And laughter, learnt of friends; and gentleness,
In hearts at peace, under an English heaven."

This one is an entire verse — that's way too long.

Example

The poet tries to find comfort in the idea of dying at war when he writes about "hearts at peace, under an English heaven."

This quotation is much better — it just uses a few words to make the point.

> Try to quote using the fewest number of words you can.
> Don't be afraid to quote a single word if it's enough to make your point.

...but do it Often

Your answer should be full of short quotations backing up your points.

You might not always be able to find the exact quotation you're looking for — but your answers will be better with a selection of good quotations.

Quotations — keep 'em short and sweet.

Phew-urgh words are better...

You don't need to quote vast chunks of writing, just the bit that makes the point. It's quicker, too.

Warm-Up Questions

Don't quote me on this, but this page might just be a great way of testing your knowledge...

Warm-Up Questions

1) Rewrite the following piece of text using your own words.

> Tanya felt like something wasn't quite right as she crept up the stairs to her room. The darkness unsettled her even more.

2) Which of these quotations could be used to back up the following point?

Tanya was afraid of the ghost.

a)
> Tanya woke up when she heard a noise outside.

b)
> Tanya saw a ghost come in through her bedroom window.

c)
> Tanya's teeth started to chatter as the ghost approached her.

d)
> The ghost wailed before disappearing into thin air.

3) Rewrite the following answer so that the quotation is embedded in the middle of the sentence. You can shorten the quotation if you need to.

> Although the ghost disappears, the author implies that it will come back later in the story — "Tanya had a feeling she hadn't seen the last of the ghost."

Worked Practice Questions

Have a look at these questions to get a better idea of what you'll be expected to do in the exam.

Worked Practice Questions

This extract is the introduction from a non-fiction book aimed at teenagers.
It is a handbook for people who want to be vegetarians.

> It all starts here — with the ultimate guide to going, being and staying veggie.
>
> This book will take you through the change from being a meatie to being a vegetarian — every step of the way. Every question answered, every doubt knocked on the head and every concern sorted.
>
> If you're already a veggie, this book will give you the confidence and knowledge to argue for your beliefs. If your parents are worried, it will put their minds at rest. If you're short of facts, you'll find them here.

1. Pick out a quotation that shows that the book contains everything the reader needs.

   "the ultimate guide"

2. Pick out a quotation that suggests the writer is talking directly to the reader.

   "this book will give you the confidence"

3. Find an example of repetition from the text. What effect does this have on the reader?

   "Every question... every doubt... every concern". The repetition of "every"

   makes it sound as though the handbook has all the information you'll need.

4. Using the quotations from the questions above, as well as any other details from the text, make a plan for the following question.

   | Q | How does the author create a reassuring tone? |

   In the exam, you'd use your plan to write a full answer.

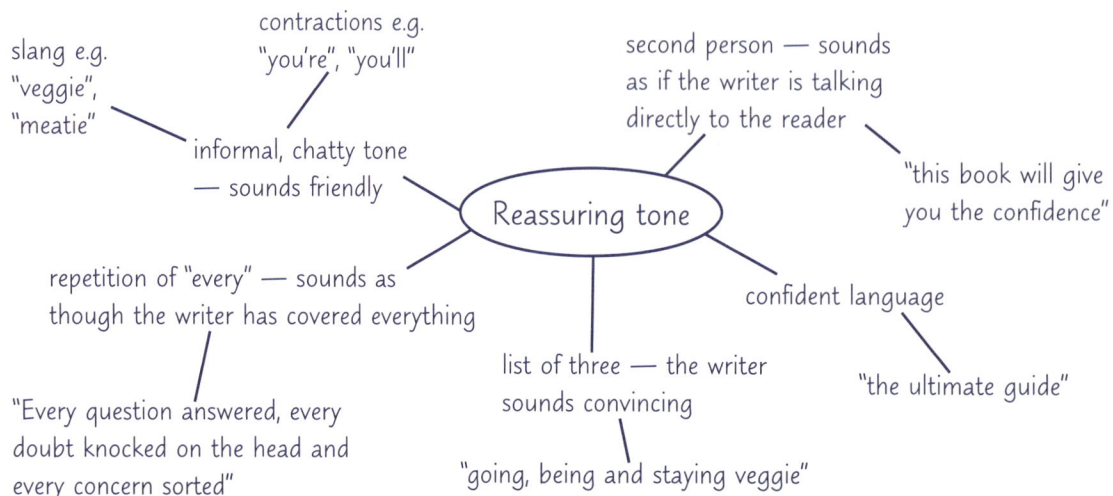

   slang e.g. "veggie", "meatie"

   contractions e.g. "you're", "you'll"

   second person — sounds as if the writer is talking directly to the reader

   informal, chatty tone — sounds friendly

   "this book will give you the confidence"

   Reassuring tone

   repetition of "every" — sounds as though the writer has covered everything

   confident language

   "Every question answered, every doubt knocked on the head and every concern sorted"

   list of three — the writer sounds convincing

   "the ultimate guide"

   "going, being and staying veggie"

Practice Questions

Read the following extract, then have a go at answering the questions about it.

Practice Questions

The following extract is adapted from Frances Hodgson Burnett's novel, *The Secret Garden*. In the extract, Mary and Dickon are meeting for the first time. Read the extract, then answer the questions that follow.

A boy was sitting under a tree, with his back against it, playing on a rough wooden pipe. He was a funny looking boy about twelve. He looked very clean and his nose turned up and his cheeks were as red as poppies and never had Mistress Mary seen such round and such blue eyes in any boy's face. And on the trunk of the tree he leaned against, a brown squirrel was clinging and watching him, and from behind a bush nearby a cock pheasant was delicately stretching his neck to peep out, and quite near him were two rabbits sitting up and sniffing with tremulous noses — and actually it appeared as if they were all drawing near to watch him and listen to the strange low little call his pipe seemed to make.

When he saw Mary he held up his hand and spoke to her in a voice almost as low as and rather like his piping.

[...]

"I'm Dickon," the boy said. "I know th'art Miss Mary."

Then Mary realised that somehow she had known at first that he was Dickon. Who else could have been charming rabbits and pheasants? He had a wide, red, curving mouth and his smile spread all over his face.

"I got up slow," he explained, "because if tha' makes a quick move it startles 'em. A body 'as to move gentle an' speak low when wild things is about."

He did not speak to her as if they had never seen each other before but as if he knew her quite well.

1. Dickon tells Mary "if tha' makes a quick move it startles 'em".
   Which of the following best describes Dickon's manner of speaking?
   a. He uses formal language.
   b. He uses non-standard English.
   c. He uses poetic language.
   d. He uses foreign words and phrases.

Practice Questions

2. Explain what each of these quotations suggests about Dickon.

    a)   "never had Mistress Mary seen such round and such blue eyes"

    ....

    b)   "they were all drawing near to watch him"

    ....

    c)   "I know th'art Miss Mary"

    ....

    d)   "When he saw Mary he held up his hand and spoke to her"

    ....

3. Make a plan for the following question in the box below. You can use the quotations
    from the question above if you want to, as well as any other details from the text.

    What impression does the writer give of Dickon in this extract?

    In the exam, you'd use your plan to write a full answer.

Summary Questions

By now you should know everything there is to know about quoting. Lucky you. Remember, there's no way of creating the perfect answer without a clear and thorough understanding of the whole of this section. And there's an easy way to work out if you've got to grips with it — test yourself on these questions, and go over the section until you can do them all. Instantly. No hesitation. Like a pro.

1) What do you have to do to back up every point you make? ☐

2) Complete this simple rule:
   "Every time you make a point, _____ it _____ with an _____." ☐

3) A good way to remember to back up your point is to:
   a) imagine that your reader is an expert on the text you're talking about,
   b) imagine that your reader has never seen the text you're talking about, or
   c) imagine that you're a field agent calling for backup. ☐

4) When you give your answer, why shouldn't you write your reasons in
   exactly the same words as the original piece of writing? ☐

5) When can you copy the words of a text exactly? ☐

6) How do you show that something's a quotation? ☐

7) Complete the sentences below.
   a) When you back up a point with a _____, you must use your own words.
   b) When you back up a point with a _____, you must copy that bit of text exactly. ☐

8) If you're quoting more than one line of poetry, when should you use this '/' symbol? ☐

9) What do you need to make sure you do when quoting from a play? ☐

10) What are the two ways in which you can give a reason and explain it with
    a quotation? ☐

11) Give one reason why quotations shouldn't be too long. ☐

12) How often should you use quotations? ☐

The Writing Exam

We met the reading exam in Section 2. Now it's time to tackle its mate — the writing exam.

You must answer **two questions** in the **Writing** paper

As you might know by now, whether you're doing the Paper 1 reading exam or the Foundation reading exam, you have to do the writing exam (Paper 2).

1) In Paper 2, there'll be a choice of four topics for you to write about. You only need to choose two of these topics, so make sure you don't write about all four.

> If you're sitting 13+ exams set by your school, the papers might be structured differently to this. Ask your teacher what your papers will look like.

2) There are various types of texts you could be asked to write, such as:

- A descriptive text or short story (p.47)
- A formal or informal letter (p.48)
- A news report or blog post (p.54-58)
- An information leaflet or report (p.54-58)
- A speech or written argument (p.59)

Spend **30 Minutes** on **each question**

1) The paper lasts 1 hour 15 minutes.

2) The entire paper is worth 50 marks — 25 marks for each question.

3) That means you'll have roughly 30 minutes for each answer, with 15 minutes spare to read the paper, plan your answers and check your work.

4) Planning your work is vital (see p.44). It'll help you to structure your answer well.

Spelling, **Punctuation** and **Grammar** are **Important**

1) The examiner will be looking out for some top-notch spelling, punctuation, grammar and vocabulary.

2) You need to work quickly in the exam, but make sure that you're careful to spell words correctly, punctuate your sentences well, and use paragraphs properly.

3) The examiner would love to see some exciting vocabulary in your answer too, so if you know a great word or phrase that would fit, then make sure you use it.

30 minutes, 25 marks — you do the maths...

Actually, don't worry about the maths — focus on the English. This section is all about how you can get some cracking marks in your 13+ English writing paper. Ready? Let's go...

Looking at the Question

You're not going to write a decent answer if you don't look carefully at the question first.

Read the Question

It's always tempting to start writing straight away, but it's not a good idea.

1) Take the time to read the question and think about what it's asking you to do.

2) Make sure you know what you're supposed to write about before you get going.

Write in the Style that the Question tells you

Always think about what kind of writing the question is asking for. For example, you might be asked to imagine you're someone else, such as a teacher, or a character in a story. You have to think about what words they would use when they write or say something.

> Prisha stood in the museum looking at the dinosaur bones. There was a sign saying, "Do not touch", but Prisha didn't see it. After a while she reached out and grabbed hold of a bone. The museum attendant quickly ran over and told her to stop.

Example

Imagine you are the museum attendant.
Write an account of the same event.　　　[25]

In this question, you're a museum attendant. You should write in the way that he or she would write, e.g. you might be angry about children mucking around in the museum.

> Children have no respect for the rules of the museum. Only today I had to stop a young girl from touching the dinosaur bones.

The style of your writing will depend on who you're writing to, why you're writing, and what kind of text a question is asking you to write.

If the question tells you to write a speech, be snappy, punchy and direct to get the reader's attention — like this.

> The faulty pelican crossing has caused ten accidents. We must take action now before someone else is injured, or even killed. Write to your local councillor at once.

If you're asked to write a formal letter of complaint, use loads of formal language, and don't forget to end it with 'Yours sincerely' or 'Yours faithfully' (see p.48 for which to use).

> Dear Mr Goodman,
>   I am writing to complain about the appalling service that I experienced whilst dining at your restaurant. My wife and I were most distressed as we had to wait two hours for our meals...

Forget the hocus pocus — focus on the question...

It may sound an obvious thing to say, but reading the question carefully is incredibly important. No matter how good your answer is, if it doesn't do what the question asks you, it's no good.

Planning Your Answer

If you don't think planning is important, think again. A good plan can mean better writing.

Plan before you start Writing

If you <u>dive straight in</u> without planning first, it'll all go <u>horribly wrong</u>.

<u>One</u> page of well <u>planned</u>, well-thought-out writing is <u>always</u> better than <u>five</u> pages written off the <u>top</u> of your <u>head</u>.

Have a <u>good think</u> about what you're going to write about <u>before</u> you start. You don't need to know <u>exactly</u> what you're going to write, but you need to have a <u>rough idea</u>.

Good writing <u>makes a point</u>. It doesn't just ramble on about nothing.

Whether you're writing a story, a description, a letter or a speech, make sure you've got <u>enough different ideas</u> for the whole thing — no waffle.

Jot Down your Points into a Rough Plan

It's a good idea to jot down a <u>plan</u> of the points you want to make <u>before</u> you start writing. That way you won't get to the end and realise you've <u>forgotten</u> something.

Example

Write an article for a magazine about an issue that's important to you. Explain why you think the issue is important. [25]

1) A plan doesn't have to be in proper sentences. It's just a <u>reminder</u> for you to use.

2) <u>Start</u> with what you think is the <u>most important</u> point. This grabs your reader's attention.

3) Try to <u>link</u> your points together. You can link smoothly from meat to treatment of animals.

4) Work out how you're going to <u>end</u> your piece. This is a positive ending — it says what we can do.

Plan: Modern farming methods

Reducing quality of soil — less food can be grown — soon we won't have enough to eat.

Risks to human health — pesticides — antibiotics in meat.

Animals treated badly — profits more important than welfare.

What we can do — buy organic.

No rambling — so no walking boots needed...

REVISION TASK

Your plan can be a bit <u>rough</u>, as long as it <u>focuses</u> on the <u>question</u> and includes your <u>main points</u>. Write your own plan for an information leaflet explaining why littering is harmful.

Structuring Your Writing

All writing follows a similar structure — it'll have a beginning, a middle and an end.

A **Good Introduction** is **Crucial**

An introduction is really important. A good one will make your reader want to read on.

Example

Do you ever dream of a better bed? If your current bed is old, hard or lumpy, it could be stopping you from getting the good night's sleep you deserve.

This is the introduction to a persuasive text that's trying to sell something. It uses a question to get the reader's attention and it makes the reader feel important.

This is the introduction to an argument. It sets out the argument clearly and uses strong language to convince the reader.

Example

I passionately believe that our school needs a breakfast club. Breakfast is the most important meal of the day. Research has proved time and time again that a good breakfast does wonders for our brains and our bodies.

Signposting sets out **What** you're going to **Say**

An introduction, especially in an essay or a speech, should set out what you're going to cover in the rest of the text. This is called signposting.

Example

Choosing to live a healthier life doesn't need to be complicated. There are three simple things you can do to improve your health: eat more fruit and vegetables, exercise regularly and eat less junk food.

This introduction clearly sets out what the text is going to cover and in what order. This way the reader knows exactly what they're going to find in the text.

The **Middle** is the **Main Bit** of your writing

The middle bit of your writing covers the main part of what you want to say. It should include all the things from your plan (see p.44) and follow the order that you set out in the introduction.

The main bit of your writing should be in clear paragraphs. Use a paragraph for each point (see p.73-75).

If you're writing to inform, argue or persuade, you should include some facts and statistics to support what you're saying.

Example

Fruit and vegetables contain lots of vitamins and nutrients that keep our bodies healthy...

Regular exercise is great for your heart and it can be loads of fun too...

Junk food is normally high in fat and sugar. Too much fat and sugar in your diet is bad for your health...

Structuring your writing makes it Easier to Understand

1) If you're writing a report, a pamphlet, or another kind of informative text, dividing your writing into clear paragraphs or sections makes it easier for the reader to understand.

2) It might also help to use headings and subheadings to structure your answer. Headings help the reader to pick out the information they need easily, so including them in your writing shows that you've thought about your audience and purpose.

A Good Ending will Impress your reader

1) The ending is the last thing your reader will read, so you want it to be memorable.

2) If it's really good, it'll give your reader a positive impression of everything you've already said.

3) If you're writing to argue or persuade, then your ending is your last chance to get your reader to agree with you, so you've got to make it first class.

Different Texts need Different Kinds of Ending

Fiction texts need endings that tie up the plot, while non-fiction texts need conclusions.

Ending a Story

A good ending ties up the loose ends of the story. The reader shouldn't be left confused about what's happened.

If you write a story about a personal experience you could end it by saying how you feel about it now.

Example

Looking back, I feel lucky that nothing really bad happened to me. I still walk home, but I have never taken that short cut again.

Ending a Persuasive Text or Speech

A clever trick is to write a sentence in your conclusion that links to what you said in your introduction. You could also finish by asking the reader to do something.

Example — Introduction

The lack of facilities is an issue which affects us all.

Example — Conclusion

This is indeed an issue that affects us all. Please petition your local MP today.

Time to wrap it up — who's got the parcel tape?

A catchy beginning, a clear middle and a memorable ending — it sounds like a tall order. But follow the advice in this section, and with plenty of practice you'll soon be writing masterpieces...

Writing Stories

It's not just non-fiction texts that need plans. Stories improve with planning too.

Plan what will Happen in your Story

It's tempting just to start by writing "Once upon a time..." and hope that you'll be able to make up what happens in your story as you go along. But that's a really bad idea.

Before you start to write your story, you should have a good idea of how it's going to end, and what's going to happen in the middle. Otherwise you'll have all sorts of problems.

Example

Write about an exciting journey you have made. It can be real or imaginary.   [25]

Plan: Going on holiday on a plane. ◄——— This plan is like a summary of the story you're going to write.

Everyone except me got very ill from the food.

Went to the cockpit — pilot was unconscious. ◄——— When you write the story, you could have two or three paragraphs about each of these points.

I talked to air traffic control over the pilot's radio and they told me what to do.

I landed the plane safely. You've planned how it's going to end, so you always know what you're aiming towards.

Everyone went to hospital — they were all fine.

Start with something Exciting

No one wants to read a story with a boring start. The beginning needs to GRAB THE READER'S ATTENTION. Start with something exciting, and the person reading your story can't help but want to read on. They'll want to find out what happens next.

Naomi moved away. The edge of the cliff crumbled and she plunged backwards.

There are many ways of grabbing the reader's attention. For example, if you start with someone speaking, the person reading your story will want to find out who they are and what they're talking about.

"Don't leave!" I cried, but the rocket was already taking off. Without it, I had no way of getting back to Earth.

You don't need to explain everything at once. Make the reader want to read on.

Grab 'em right at the start — then don't let 'em go...

REVISION TIP

If you're struggling to find interesting ways to start your stories, have a look at the opening lines of your favourite books — think about how the author grabs the reader's attention.

Writing Letters

The exam could ask you to write a formal or informal letter, so make sure you know the difference.

Use Formal Language in a Formal Letter

1) When you write a formal letter, you have to use a more formal style.

2) This style is used in important documents, e.g. a letter from school, a job application.

3) Here are some key features of letters written in a formal style:

- They might have a detached tone.
- They often use more complex vocabulary and avoid slang terms.
- They avoid using contractions.
- They don't use exclamation marks.

A contraction is a short form of a word (see p.83).

Informal Letters use casual, Chatty Language

1) When you write an informal letter, you can use a more informal style.

2) This style is more appropriate when you're writing to someone that you know.

3) Here are some key features of letters written in an informal style:

- They often sound like they're talking to the person you're writing to — the letter sounds more natural.
- They still use proper sentences even though they are written in a more friendly way.
- They use contractions, chatty language and exclamation marks.

Make sure you End your letter Appropriately

1) For a formal letter, if you know the name of the recipient, end it with 'Yours sincerely'.

2) If you don't know the name of the recipient, end the letter with 'Yours faithfully'. You would do this if you addressed the letter 'Dear Sir/Madam', like when writing to a company.

Example

I hope that you will resolve the issue as soon as possible.

Yours faithfully,

It's a good idea to end a letter of complaint by reminding the reader that they're supposed to do something.

Don't forget to put a comma after 'Yours faithfully' and 'Yours sincerely'.

Informal writing doesn't mean it's poorly written

Make sure that any letter that you write completes the task in the question and is written in the most appropriate style. Even if the letter is to a friend, you need to make sure the letter is written well.

Correcting Mistakes

If you spot a mistake, don't panic — you'll know what to do once you've read this stuff...

Cross Out your mistakes Neatly

1) Don't worry if you find a mistake when you check your work.
   As long as your corrections are clear, you won't lose any marks.

2) If it's just one word or a short phrase that's wrong, cross it out neatly and write the correct word above it.

3) Always cross out the whole word or phrase, not just the wrong letters.

4) You should never write on top of a word to correct it — it's much clearer if you cross out the old word and write the new word above.

Don't use correction fluid or eraser pens — they look messy.

Example

The author uses a series of metafors to describe the rain.

Here's the mistake you need to correct.

Example

The author uses a series of metafors to describe the rain.

Your writing won't be clear if you write over what you've already written.

Example

The author uses a series of
metaphors
~~metafors~~ to describe the rain.

This is better — draw a clear line through your mistake and write the whole word above it.

Always make sure the examiner can read your writing.

Use a Double Strike to show a New Paragraph

If you've forgotten to start a new paragraph, use a double strike (like this '//') to show where the new paragraph should begin.

You usually show the start of a paragraph with a new line and an indent.

Each new point needs a new paragraph. Your plan should show where each one starts.

Example

Our community garden is an important place where people of all ages can relax and enjoy nature in a safe environment. We believe that the garden should be given £200 so that we can purchase a brand new bench. //Another organisation that deserves money from the council is the local sports club. They want to build a new indoor tennis centre so that people can play tennis throughout the year.

Use a double strike to show that a new paragraph should start here.

Use an **Asterisk** to add **Extra Information**

If you realise that you've <u>missed something out</u>, the first thing to do is decide whether there's enough <u>space</u> to write the missing bit <u>above</u> the line you've already written.

If you <u>can</u>, write the missing bit <u>above</u> the line with a '∧' to show <u>exactly where</u> it should go.

Example

was
The door creaked open, but there∧nobody there.

This shows that the word
'was' is <u>missing</u> after 'there'.

If the bit you've missed out <u>won't</u> fit <u>above</u> the line, use an <u>asterisk</u> (like this *) to show <u>where</u> it should go. Write the missing stuff at the <u>end</u> of your essay with an asterisk next to it.

Example

The <u>asterisk</u> shows that something is <u>missing</u> here.

Brenda sprinted towards the station, but it was too late. * She turned back towards home, frustrated, and with Diego's brown leather briefcase still in her hand.

* Diego was already sitting on a train, hurtling through the countryside.

Put the asterisk <u>next to</u> the words you want to <u>add</u>.

> Too many asterisks can be confusing. Making a plan at the start will help you to avoid missing out important points.

Cross Out anything you **Don't** want to be **Marked**

If you don't want the examiner to read something, just <u>cross it out neatly</u>.

The same goes for parts of your answer that you decide are <u>wrong</u> — if you want to get rid of a <u>paragraph</u> in the middle of your answer, cross it out <u>clearly</u>. You can <u>replace</u> it with a new paragraph using an <u>asterisk</u> and a <u>new paragraph</u> at the end.

Try not to cross out too much stuff — you might get marks for some of it.

Whatever you do, <u>don't</u> start <u>scribbling</u> things out willy nilly. It'll make your answer look really <u>messy</u>.

> Always make sure your answers are clear and tidy.

Correct me if I'm wrong, but this seems important...

Why yes it is — thank you ever so much for saying so. The main thing to remember is that <u>everyone makes mistakes</u>, but you'll do well if you can <u>correct</u> your mistakes <u>clearly</u> and <u>neatly</u>.

Warm-Up and Worked Practice Questions

Here are some warm-up questions to ease you into exam mode.

Warm-Up Questions

1) What is signposting?

2) What is different about the language used in a formal letter compared to the language used in an informal letter?

3) A double strike can be used to show where a new paragraph should start. True or false?

This worked answer shows you how you could plan your answer if you're asked to write a story.

Worked Practice Question

This is the start of a story called 'The Great Mystery'.

The Great Mystery

Ayesha carefully opened the battered door in front of her, flinching ever so slightly as it creaked. She'd been hearing strange noises coming from this abandoned house for a couple of weeks and had finally mustered enough courage to do some investigating. As she crept into the dimly lit entrance hall, she noticed that everything was coated in a thick layer of dust.

1. Write the rest of the story above in your own words.

In the exam, you'd use your plan to write a full answer.

PLAN

BEGINNING — Ayesha explores the house, finds interesting and unusual items. She pockets a few of the more interesting items, thinking that she could find out more about them later.

MIDDLE — She starts to hear a strange scratching noise coming from somewhere within the house. Looks through each downstairs room, growing increasingly nervous as the noise continues. She realises that the noise is coming from upstairs.

END — She goes into an upstairs room and discovers what is making the noise. It turns out to be a cat with a litter of kittens, living in the upstairs bedroom.

Practice Questions

Try your hand at these questions to see what you've learnt. Remember — in the exam, you'd need to write a detailed response to each one, so take your time and don't try them all at once.

Practice Questions

1. Write a letter to your friend describing a recent holiday.
   You should:
   - say where you went
   - describe what you did
   - explain what you did and didn't enjoy.

2. Write the opening to a story with the title 'The New Arrival'.

3. Write a blog post informing readers what there is to do in your local area.

4. Write a description of your perfect beach. The beach can be either real or imaginary.
   You should:
   - describe the beach's main features
   - describe the weather and location
   - explain why you think it is perfect.

Imagine this notice went up in your school.

> ### NOTICE TO ALL STUDENTS
>
> Following the consistent damaging of books belonging to the school library, it has been decided that no pupils will be allowed into the library during lunchtime or after school. Pupils may only enter the library when they have a lesson there or are supervised by a teacher.
>
> This rule will be enforced from now on and applies to all students.

5. Write a letter to your head teacher persuading them to reverse their decision.
   You should:
   - explain why you believe the new rule is wrong
   - explain why having access to the library is important
   - suggest ways in which the books can be better protected.

Summary Questions

You wouldn't think there were so many tricks to doing something as simple as writing, but trust me — knowing all the stuff in this section will make a huge difference. Just don't be a bird-brain and think you can wing it. Go over this section till you can answer every one of these questions.

1) What should you do instead of starting to write straight away at the start of an exam? ☐

2) Explain what kind of style you would write in if you were each of these people:
   a) a head teacher   b) a rap musician   c) an author of a romantic novel ☐

3) A speech should be:
   a) long and rambling   b) punchy and direct   c) in a foreign language ☐

4) Which of these are good ideas for writing a plan for your answer?
   a) Always write in full sentences.
   b) Start with the most important point.
   c) Start with the least important point.
   d) Try to link your points together in a smooth argument.
   e) Don't bother with planning an ending — it'll probably change anyway. ☐

5) When making your main points, you shouldn't bother following
   the order that you laid out in the introduction. True or false? ☐

6) A text that aims to inform the reader contains:
   a) long, elegant descriptions,
   b) lots of facts, or
   c) lots of your own opinions. ☐

7) It's a really effective idea to link the conclusion of your persuasive writing with:
   a) something you said in your introduction,
   b) something you said to your grandma last Tuesday, or
   c) something your mates have written in their essays. ☐

8) When you're planning a story, is it best to:
   a) not plan the ending, so you can decide at the last minute what you want to do, or
   b) plan the ending so you know what you're aiming towards? ☐

9) Your story should begin with:
   a) a brief summary of the characters and plot,
   b) something exciting, or
   c) a long speech from the main character about what they had for lunch. ☐

10) How should you end a formal letter in the following situations?
    a) When you know the name of the recipient.
    b) When you don't know the name of the recipient. ☐

11) What would you use an asterisk for in your answer? ☐

Writing to Persuade and Argue

It's quite likely that you'll have to write a text in favour of an opinion, or to persuade someone.

Arguing and Persuading are quite similar

1) Writing to <u>argue</u> is about getting people to <u>agree with your opinions</u> and showing why other people's opinions are <u>wrong</u> (or at least not as good as yours).

2) Writing to <u>persuade</u> is when you encourage the reader to <u>do something</u> or to think in the <u>same way</u> you do. Persuading can be a lot like trying to <u>sell</u> something.

3) When you're writing to argue or persuade, you need to give <u>clear</u> and <u>convincing</u> reasons to support what you say. The techniques on the following pages are useful for both <u>arguing</u> and <u>persuading</u> — so learn them well.

Work out the Opposite view — then say it's Wrong

If you're trying to <u>persuade</u> someone to do something or <u>argue</u> an opinion, it's useful to look at it from <u>the other point of view</u>.

Think about why people might <u>not</u> agree with you — then work out how to <u>prove them wrong</u>.

Example

Here's how you might plan a speech trying to <u>persuade</u> people to <u>support</u> a <u>ban</u> on fox hunting.

Notes: Reasons why people disagree with banning fox hunting

1. Countryside jobs — but few people would be affected

2. Need to cull foxes — but there are more humane ways

3. Tradition — but so was bear-baiting

These are reasons it should <u>NOT</u> be banned.

Here's how you can say these reasons are <u>wrong</u>.

And here's how you could write out one of those points.

<u>Why fox hunting should be banned</u>

Supporters of fox hunting say that it's a tradition. But in the past, it was also traditional to bait bears. Times change, and society moves on. Just because something is traditional is no reason to keep doing it.

Show that you've <u>thought</u> about what your opponents say and that you still <u>disagree</u> with them. That way you'll have more chance of <u>convincing</u> other people that <u>your</u> view is <u>right</u>.

Exaggerate your **Good Points**

It might sound a bit unfair to exaggerate how good your own arguments are. But don't worry — everyone does it. If you don't exaggerate, people might think your points are weak.

This works really well in articles, speeches, and also in texts that are trying to sell a product.

Make your points with style, and use a few facts and statistics to make them more convincing.

Example 1 — Rubbish

Global warming could be quite a problem. Some scientists think the earth is getting warmer quite quickly. That might mean that a fair bit of farmland turns into desert, so people might not have enough food.

Words like "massive", "frightening" and "huge" are stronger than words like "quite" or "a fair bit".

It says "many scientists" instead of "some".

It says "will" and "huge areas" instead of "might" and "a fair bit".

It talks about "billions of people" instead of just saying "people".

Using "starve" is scarier than "not have enough food".

Example 2 — Good

Global warming is a massive threat to the very future of humanity. Many scientists believe the earth is getting warmer at a frightening rate. If this continues, huge areas of farmland will turn into desert, causing billions of people to starve.

Be careful, though — you're allowed to exaggerate, but you're not allowed to lie. You can't say things that aren't true, like "global warming will cause aliens to take over the Earth".

If you say things that obviously aren't true, people won't trust the rest of your arguments.

Make your **Opponents** sound **Unreasonable**

You can also exaggerate what people who disagree say, to make them sound unreasonable. It's a great tactic when writing an argument...

Putting your opponents' point of view in your own words is a good way of making them sound bad.

Example

Some businessmen believe we have no responsibility to the environment. They think it doesn't matter if we keep on churning out deadly greenhouse gases. All they care about is making profits.

You can be harsh — as long as you don't tell any actual lies.

10 out of 10 for exagge — a high exagge-rating...

Exaggeration is a crucial trick when you're arguing or persuading. You can use it to make yourself sound good, and make your opponents sound bad. But make sure you don't lie.

Writing to Explain

Writing to explain means giving people an explanation. It's not rocket science.

Explanations tell your audience **Five Main Things**

If you're writing to explain, you basically want your readers to understand as much as possible about your topic. Start by making sure you cover these five key points:

The WHAT...	...the HOW...	...the WHERE...

What is going on?   How is it happening?   Where is it happening?

...the WHEN..	...and the WHY.

When is it happening?   Why is it happening?

Explanations can take **Many Forms**

When you explain something, break down the detail of a topic to present it clearly. Just like revision, things are easier to understand when explained in smallish chunks.

Think carefully about who your writing is aimed at and adapt your writing style to this audience.

Here are some examples of "writing to explain" questions that could be in your exam:

An explanation of a personal experience or ambition.
→ Choose a time when you felt a very strong emotion and explain why you felt this way.

An explanation of what might happen in the future.
→ Explain what life might be like in the year 2500.

An explanation of a journey you went on.
→ Write a report about a school trip you went on. Explain where you went and what you saw.

REVISION TIP

What? Why? How? Is this some sort of investigation?

When you're writing to explain, make a list of the main points you want to cover before you start writing. It'll make it a lot easier to structure your answer and make it interesting.

Writing to Inform

When you write to inform, you do what it says on the tin — you give people information.

Writing to inform Tells the reader Facts

If you're writing to inform, you need to tell the reader something as clearly and effectively as possible.

This might involve talking about personal experiences (e.g. a significant incident in your life) or something you feel strongly about. You must make sure that you keep the emphasis on giving out clear facts in an organised structure. Avoid opinions or waffle.

Your style might be formal or informal. Make sure you think about your audience when you decide which style you need.

Informative language is Clear and Factual

1) Informative writing needs to be snappy and direct.

2) Make sure you stick to the facts and keep things impersonal.

3) Try and keep your sentences as short and as straightforward as possible.

Example

I reckon global warming is a big problem, as it causes loads of environmental problems.

This answer is too personal. It's also really vague and rambling.

Example

Global warming has led to a rise in the Earth's average temperature. Consequences of this include droughts, hurricanes, fires and rising sea levels.

This is loads better.

There are Loads of Examples of Writing to Inform

Here are some different types of writing that you might be asked to do for an inform question.

A magazine article or blog post informing people about environmental problems.

A letter to a pen-friend telling them about where you live.

A report about a school or club event.

An information leaflet for a local museum.

Well, that all seems very informative...

Writing to inform is easy as long as you don't get over-excited. Your language should be calm and factual. Avoid giving opinions and stick to a clear structure. Don't make things personal.

Writing to Advise

When you're writing to advise, you want to help the reader with some gems of wisdom.

There are many different Types of Advice

From 'how to quit smoking' leaflets to agony aunt pages, written advice is everywhere.

Writing to advise is a bit weird — it's a mixture of writing to inform and writing to persuade. For example, a leaflet on quitting smoking needs to persuade people to quit and inform them how to do it.

There are various types of advice you could be asked to write, such as:

MAGAZINE AND NEWSPAPER ARTICLES
e.g. an article about how to eat more
healthily or how to look after a pet

SPEECHES
e.g. to advise pupils how to
revise for exams effectively

Written advice needs to be Reassuring

1) Written advice has got to get the reader's attention — a good heading would do the trick.

2) It's got to be clear what the advice is about (e.g. from the heading) so that people can decide whether or not they want to read it. A leaflet on healthy eating is no good if it looks like a leaflet on bike maintenance...

3) Finally, if the reader is going to take your advice, they need to feel that you understand the issue thoroughly. You can convince them by using a reassuring tone throughout the text:

Great Exam Advice

Example

Don't worry if it takes a while for leaves to appear on the shoots — plants all grow at different rates. Just make sure you keep them well watered.

Written advice suggests what Action to take

So... when you're writing your advice, you need to get the reader's attention, reassure them about what they're doing, and then, finally, you can actually give them your advice.

You need to suggest to the reader what courses of action they could take.

You could give them a range of different options so they have some choice.

Then it's all up to the reader to take your advice... or not.

Example

You need to find a warm place to leave the plants. This could be:

- a conservatory
- an airing cupboard
- on a high shelf

My parents call it advising — I call it nagging...

State what you're going to advise on, reassure the reader and then give them an action plan. With these three little steps you too can fulfil your life's ambition and become an agony aunt.

Writing a Speech

Speeches need to be interesting and informative. They are written to persuade an audience.

Speeches are Written to be Spoken

1) It's really important to remember that what you're writing is intended to be <u>said aloud</u>.

2) This means it doesn't need to be as <u>formal</u> as some other writing tasks.

3) You do need to use correct <u>grammar</u>, though.

4) Try to <u>impress</u> your audience with a range of vocabulary that will grab their <u>attention</u>.

Make your writing Memorable

It's essential that your speech <u>stands out</u>. There are loads of things you can do to make sure your speech comes alive...

- Use <u>interesting similes and metaphors</u>.

- Add in some <u>rhetorical questions</u> to get the audience's attention. These are questions that <u>don't</u> expect a <u>response</u>, and they can make the audience <u>think</u> about your points and <u>engage</u> with them.

- Using <u>repetition</u> is a good way of <u>reinforcing</u> your points.

- <u>Lists of three</u> are really <u>persuasive</u> devices. They make you sound <u>certain</u>, e.g. 'You should buy this house because it is available, attractive <u>and</u> affordable."

Think about Purpose and Audience

The point of a speech is to <u>persuade</u>. It needs to be <u>striking</u> but also easy to <u>understand</u>. Use <u>emotive language</u> to write a <u>powerful</u> and <u>engaging</u> speech. Using "I" and "you" will also help you appeal <u>directly</u> to your audience.

> Emotive language is language that has an emotional effect on the reader.

Don't bore your audience with too much jargon or slang.

> From the beginning of this fiscal year, this company has adopted a belt-and-braces approach to market capitalisation, dictated by a 3% dip in share-price...

There's too much jargon in this speech...

> Ladies and gentlemen, have you ever wondered why hip-hop music is so popular? I love hip-hop because of its groovy beat, its rhythmic feel and its iconic artists...

...but this one is a lot easier to understand, so it's more engaging.

REVISION TASK

"...and so my message to you all is: learn this page!"

Write a short speech presenting your views on whether school uniforms should exist. Once you've finished, read it to a friend and try to persuade them that your perspective is right.

Writing from Your Point of View

Writing from your own viewpoint can be a bit tricky, but this advice will help you get going.

It could be a **Memory** or **Personal Opinion**

Think about who you're writing for and the purpose of the text you are writing.
If you can write in any form, think about what's best for getting your feelings across.

1. Think about the specific details or events that have led you to have a particular opinion.

2. Include lots of personal anecdotes — you can make them up if you have to, but it's easier if you've got some real ones you can relate to.

3. Don't be shy about expressing strong emotions like fear or pain — it'll make your writing a lot more powerful.

4. Don't just say how things look. Think about how things sound, smell, feel and taste.

Have a look at these **Example Tasks**

Some writing tasks, like informal letters and speeches, will naturally involve personal feelings.

Example

Think of a funny moment from your childhood. Write about it in an entertaining way. [25]

Direct spoken question grabs the audience's attention.

A dramatic description sets the scene — remember to use other senses too.

"Where's Dad gone?" asked my brother, looking back to where Dad should have been. We were on our annual walk to Glenbiggle Castle, through the marshy fields to the majestic, imposing, grey stone ruins. If I'm honest, I never usually enjoyed the walk, but this year was different — Dad had slipped over, and reappeared covered from head-to-toe in thick brown mud...

Using specific details makes the text more personal.

Confiding in the reader will help them engage with the story.

Example

Write about what, in your experience, makes a good friend. [25]

A chatty, first-person style is perfect for the purpose and audience of this text.

I couldn't believe that Yuna had made such a sacrifice for me. We'd only known each other for three months, but if it hadn't been for Yuna's selfless quick-thinking, I dread to think what might have happened to the rest of...

Use snappy phrases to get a lot of information into a few words.

I've got a photographic memory...

I just haven't had it developed yet... Whether you're writing about a memory or an opinion, remember the green boxes at the top of this page. Use all your senses to write a really interesting answer.

Warm-Up and Worked Practice Questions

These warm-up questions should get you firing on all cylinders.

Warm-Up Questions

1) Why is it useful to exaggerate your good points when writing a speech or an article?

2) When you're writing to inform, you should include lots of:
   a) personal opinions.
   b) persuasive devices.
   c) figurative language.
   d) factual information.

3) "If you find that you're tired all the time, there's very little you can do about it." Why is this a bad example of writing to advise?

4) Why is emotive language important when writing a speech?

Have a look at this worked answer for a question about writing to persuade.

Worked Practice Question

1. Write an article for your school magazine about unhealthy eating in school. You should try to persuade other pupils to take the issue seriously, and suggest what action should be taken.

Starting with a question engages the reader straight away.

Do you want to be unhealthy? No, neither do I, but from the way the newspapers carry on you'd think all young people want to do is eat themselves into an early grave. It's time to realise that the problem starts with the disgraceful standard of school dinners.

We all know what the problem is. The school dinners on offer are tasteless, unwholesome and usually cold. Alongside the dinners, unlimited supplies of crisps, chocolate and fizzy drinks are available from the vending machines, which causes mountains of litter. Our dining hall is more like a railway station than somewhere to enjoy a meal. It's crowded, noisy and uncomfortable and they herd us through like cattle. It's no wonder we try not to think about what we're eating.

Use 'lists of three'.

Exaggeration makes your points more forceful.

Use comparisons.

The answer continues on the next page...

Practice Questions

> *Get the readers on your side by saying 'we' and 'our'.* →
>
> So what can we do to change the situation and save ourselves from an unhealthy future? There need to be some major changes to the quality of both the food and the eating conditions in our school. We must demand a wider range of healthy foods such as salads, fresh fruit and vegetables and vegetarian options rather than chips, burgers and more chips. We need to put pressure on our school, through the school council, to provide us with a more comfortable dining room with better seating and more information about the food on offer. Most importantly, we need to make healthier choices ourselves. If it's all there for us, we'll have no excuse.
>
> *Finish by knocking down the main objection.* →
>
> Some people will say that these changes will be too expensive, but surely picking up the bill for the unhealthy adults we could become would be even more expensive in the end. If we can show our school that we want to take our health seriously, perhaps our school will take us seriously and give us the school dinners that we need.
>
> ← *Remember to end on a positive note.*

Now it's your turn to have a go. See how you get on with these practice questions.

Practice Questions

1. Write a letter to your teacher on behalf of your class, persuading them to stop setting homework on Fridays.

2. You are asked to write a speech to be performed at your school's open evening. You should argue that it would be better for students to walk or cycle to school instead of being driven by their parents.

3. A new sports centre has just opened in your town. Write an article for a local magazine to inform residents about the centre and what's on offer there.

Summary Questions

Hoorah, you've nearly completed the section on writing features. Only one final hurdle before you can make your escape — the tiny matter of a few Summary Questions. Make sure you can answer all of these before you move on. If you get some wrong, go back and check you understand everything. Then try the questions again. Once you can whizz through them without batting an eyelid, it's time to take a well-deserved break.

1) Why is it a good idea to look at your topic from the opposite point of view when you are arguing or persuading? ☐

2) Which of these would be the best sentence to include in an argument against fox hunting?
    a) Fox hunting is responsible for the deaths of a few foxes every year.
    b) Every year, fox hunting results in the violent murder of thousands of innocent foxes.
    c) Last year, fox hunters used three-headed spiders to kill over eighteen billion foxes. ☐

3) Name the five main things that explanations should tell the audience. ☐

4) Informative writing is usually made up of super-long sentences with loads of opinion and exaggeration. True or false? ☐

5) I am writing a leaflet telling people how best to look after their pet camel. Am I writing to:
    a) inform   b) persuade   c) argue? ☐

6) Mrs Sue Perior wants to write a letter to her friend, advising her about how to deal with money troubles. What should she do in her writing to show she understands her friend's situation? ☐

7) If you're writing to advise you should:
    a) tell the person you feel really sorry for them and you don't know how to help,
    b) tell the person exactly what to do and threaten to harass them if they don't, or
    c) give the person a range of possible courses of action and let them choose which one they prefer. ☐

8) Which of these devices will help to make your speeches memorable?
    a) exciting similes and metaphors
    b) technical jargon
    c) long, unstructured ramblings about your feelings on the subject
    d) rhetorical questions
    e) repetition ☐

9) List three things you should do when you're writing about a memory or personal opinion. ☐

Use Different Words

A good way to make your writing more interesting is to use lots of different words.

Use **Different Words** for the **Same Thing**

English has lots of words that mean the <u>same thing</u> as other words. That sounds a bit pointless. But it's actually <u>really handy</u>. Writing is very <u>dull</u> if it uses the same words all the time.

Have a look at these two pieces of writing and you'll see what I mean.

Different words which mean the same thing are called synonyms.

Example — dull

I went to a nice Indian restaurant. The waiters were nice to us and the walls were painted in a nice shade of red. I had an onion bhaji to start with and it was really nice. Then I had a nice curry. Later, the waiters brought us mints, which was nice of them.

It may be 'correctly' written and make sense, but it's dead <u>boring</u> — the word '<u>nice</u>' is in it again and again.

This is <u>loads better</u>. It's exactly the same piece of writing except it uses lots of <u>different</u> words instead of "nice", so it seems more <u>interesting</u>.

Example — ace

I went to a great Indian restaurant. The waiters were friendly to us and the walls were painted in a lovely shade of red. I had an onion bhaji to start with and it was really tasty. Then I had a delicious curry. Later, the waiters brought us mints, which was good of them.

It's easy to fall into the trap of using the same word all the time — especially <u>adjectives</u> like "<u>nice</u>" or "<u>weird</u>". You've got to keep an eye out and make sure you don't do it.

Look out for **Verbs** as well as **Adjectives**

There are oodles of <u>different</u> verbs too.

Look at this little piece of writing. It becomes a lot more interesting just by adding two <u>new verbs</u> instead of repeating "ran" three times.

I ran to the post box with a letter, then I ran to the shop for some chocolate. After that I ran home so I wasn't late for tea.

I ran to the post box with a letter, then I hurried to the shop for some chocolate. After that I raced home so I wasn't late for tea.

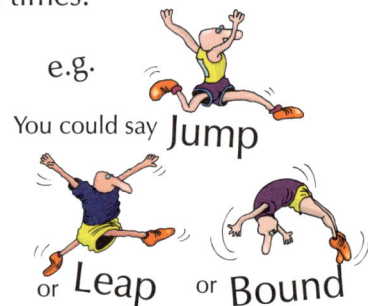

e.g.
You could say Jump
or Leap   or Bound

Use <u>different</u> words whenever you can — they make your writing <u>tons better</u>.

Clever words really Stand Out

Using <u>different</u> words is a good start.
If you can use <u>different and clever</u> words, you're laughing teacakes.

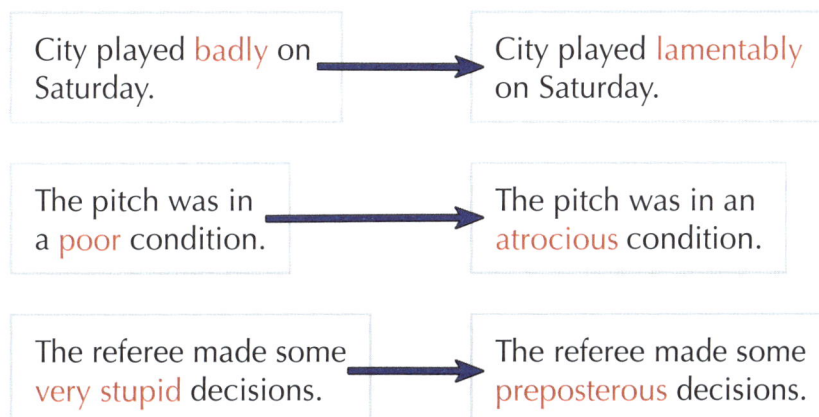

City played badly on Saturday.	→ City played lamentably on Saturday.
The pitch was in a poor condition.	→ The pitch was in an atrocious condition.
The referee made some very stupid decisions.	→ The referee made some preposterous decisions.

You can't use long fancy words <u>all</u> the time — that'd just sound <u>daft</u>.
But you'll get better marks if you throw them in <u>now and then</u>.
So remember this rule:

> Every <u>now and then</u>, try to replace a <u>short</u> and <u>simple</u> word with a <u>long</u> and <u>clever</u> one.

Of course, you have to know some <u>clever words</u> before you can use them. Get into the habit of <u>looking up</u> words you don't know in the <u>dictionary</u>. You really can't know too many words.

Use a Dictionary to help you Develop your Vocabulary

1) Spelling is <u>really important</u>. Using a clever word is like doing a trick on a skateboard — it's only really impressive if you get it right.

2) If you're not sure how to spell a word, check it in the dictionary. Then try to <u>learn</u> the spelling for the next time you need it.

3) And one last thing — <u>DON'T</u> use a long word if you're <u>not sure</u> what it means.

Use long words? — OK, wooooorrdddsssss...

REVISION TIP

The more impressive a word, the harder it can be to spell. You can work around this by keeping a list of all the long words you struggle to spell and testing yourself regularly.

Don't Be Boring

Here are a couple more tricks that'll help you make your writing more interesting.

Don't use "And" and "Then" too much

This is something loads of people do, but it makes your writing a great big yawn.

I went to the beach and I put on my trunks and I walked to the sea and the water was warm and I swam for an hour.

Instead of using "and" all the time, try to use commas and full stops.

I went to the beach, put on my trunks and walked to the sea. The water was warm. I swam for an hour.

It's OK to use "and" and "then" sometimes — but not too much.

We went to the bank then we had a coffee and then we went back to the car. Then we drove to the supermarket and did some shopping, then we drove home.

Changing the word order helps you not to use "then" all the time.

After going to the bank, we had a coffee. Then we went back to the car and drove to the supermarket. We did some shopping and drove home.

Don't start all your sentences the Same Way

This is another thing that makes your writing dull and boring.

There was a chill in the air as Jo walked towards the house. There was nobody around. There was a big oak door and Jo knocked on it. There was a scream from inside the house.

This says the same things, but in a more interesting way...

There was a chill in the air as Jo walked towards the house. Nobody was around. Jo knocked on the big oak door. A scream came from inside.

Think of different ways to start your sentences. It gets easier with practice, and it makes your writing much more interesting to read.

Use a **Variety** of **Short** and **Long** sentences

Sometimes a short sentence works best and sometimes a long one does. Neither of them work well all of the time. It's best to use a variety of different lengths.

Example

I needed to catch a train which left at one o'clock and I checked my watch and I was late so I decided to run, but the streets were busy and I kept having to dodge people. Finally I crossed the road and got to the station where I saw the train hadn't left, so I looked at my watch again and it was fast.

The first example uses all long sentences, and the second example uses all short sentences. They're both as dull as dishwater because there's no variety.

Example

I needed to catch a train. It left at one o'clock. I checked my watch. I was late. I decided to run. The streets were busy. I kept having to dodge people. It seemed to take ages. Finally I got to the station. The train hadn't left. I looked at my watch again. It was fast.

But with some long and some short sentences, this passage is far more interesting.

Example

I was walking to the station. I needed to catch a train which left at one o'clock. I checked my watch and I was late so I decided to run, but the streets were busy and I kept having to dodge people, which slowed me down. Finally I crossed the road and got to the station, where I saw the train hadn't left. I looked at my watch again. It was fast.

Long sentences are often effective for creating interesting descriptions.

Short sentences often add suspense or increase the pace of the action.

Don't use too many **Clichés** — they get **Boring**

1) Some figures of speech are used so often that they become boring — they're called clichés.

2) You hear them a lot when people are talking about sport.

| The atmosphere is electric. | I'm as sick as a parrot. | They don't pull any punches. |

3) You can get away with using some clichés in your writing, but don't use too many — people will think you haven't got anything original to say.

Hunting wild pigs — nope, that'd be 'boaring'...

These things make your writing boring: using "and" and "then" too much, starting your sentences the same way, and using all long sentences or all short sentences. Just don't do it.

Adjectives

Adjectives are great for making your writing more interesting.

Describe things with Adjectives

1) Adjectives are describing words.

2) They're a quick and easy way to spice up your writing.

Just one little adjective can completely change the impression you get from a sentence.

I ate a meal.	I ate a delicious meal.	I ate a disgusting meal.

And with three or four adjectives, you can really start to build up a picture.

I ate a delicious, sumptuous, lovingly prepared meal.	I ate a disgusting, rancid, undercooked meal.

But don't do this every time or it'll get a bit dull.

Adjectives paint a Picture

Have a look at this piece of writing. It's the adjectives that really tell you what this place is like. Without them you wouldn't get much of an idea at all.

Jordios is a quiet, sleepy village on the remote island of Toonos, 40 miles from Athens. Miles of unspoilt, sandy beaches stretch along the deserted coastline. The air is thick with the sweet smell of tall, elegant pine trees.

Rickety wooden fishing boats set off every morning from the small, picturesque harbour. In the evenings the locals gather in the cosy, welcoming tavernas for a friendly chat over a refreshing drink, and a game of table football.

Jug Suppliers — they give you pitchers...

Adjectives are a great way of describing things effectively. Putting them in your writing is like using herbs and spices when you're cooking. They make everything a bit tastier.

Comparisons

Another good way to describe something is to compare it to something else.

Less than, More than, the Least, the Most...

1) Comparisons are a great way to build up a picture of something.

2) They sound interesting and they make the text more engaging for the reader.

Amaia felt sick. Her face went green.	→ Amaia felt sick. Her face went greener than an iceberg lettuce.
It was very cold.	→ It was colder than an Arctic winter.
He was very bad at beach volleyball.	→ He was the worst beach volleyball player I had ever seen.
She was reliable.	→ She was the most reliable student in the whole school.

3) The key to making a good comparison is to pick something sensible. It's no good saying "it was colder than a pair of scissors", or "Amaia's face went as green as a doorbell".

Careful — don't write "More Better"

When you're making a comparison, you must EITHER say "more... than" or "the most...". Alternatively, with some words, you can use the form of the word that ends in "er" or "est". DON'T EVER DO BOTH.

You are more intelligent than a brick.

NOT "more intelligenter". ← "Intelligenter" isn't a word. Use a dictionary if you're unsure of a word.

You are the most sporty person I know.

NOT "most sportiest".

Timo is the cleverest boy in school.

NOT the "most cleverest".

Suzanne is prettier than her sister.

NOT "more prettier".

This rented house is the smallest — it's 'leased'...

Comparisons are another top way of making your writing more interesting — they're the greatest. But don't get confused — you can use more/most, or you can use the "er"/"est" ending. Not both.

Warm-Up Questions

After that spine-tingling, rip-roaring, joy-inducing (you get the gist) section, it's time for you to put what you've learned to the test by answering some warm-up questions.

Warm-Up Questions

1) What can you do instead of using 'and' and 'then' all the time in your writing?

2) Give two verbs which could sensibly replace the underlined verbs in the passage below.
   "I'm completely exhausted," said Kesia, struggling to catch her breath.
   "This is so boring," said Milo, low enough so that Carlos wouldn't hear.
   "Come on guys! Not much longer to the top of the mountain," said Carlos.

3) Match up the adjectives on the left with the most suitable noun on the right.
   a) blazing   message
   b) immense   sunlight
   c) bewildering   mountain

4) Using clichés all the time shows you're being imaginative. True or false?

5) Pick out the three sentences you think your teacher would be most impressed by:
   a) The band stopped playing and we all turned to face the bride and groom.
   b) He picked up the battered, grimy book and brushed the dust off the wrinkled spine.
   c) After a bone-shaking journey, the bus gasped to a halt beside a deserted building.
   d) The twins looked at each other, nodded and pressed the button.
   e) I had never seen such a hairy, flea-bitten, pitiful mongrel in all my life.

6) Match these beginnings and endings so that the comparisons make sense.
   a) She smiled like   a biscuit and a cake in one.
   b) It made a sound like   a crocodile with a good dentist.
   c) He was as lazy as   two trumpets and a sick donkey.
   d) It tasted like   a sloth sleeping in a tree.

7) Which of these two versions of the same story is better, and why?
   a) *She stopped. She saw nothing. Then, the sounds began. The whispering*
      and rustling and pattering sounds which suddenly surrounded
      her drove her further into the forest, running for her life.
   b) *She stopped but there was nothing and then the sounds began which were*
      whispering and rustling and pattering sounds which suddenly surrounded
      her and drove her further into the forest and made her run for her life.

8) Which of the following sentences makes a comparison correctly?
   a) Ursula is more stronger than a bear.
   b) Rory has the most loyalest dog ever.
   c) Masja is politer than her brother.

Practice Questions

Now have a go at writing some texts — this will really help you to prepare for your writing exam.

Practice Questions

1. Write a story with the title 'The Secret Passageway'.

2. Imagine that scientists have just discovered a new kind of animal.
   Write an article for your school newspaper about the discovery.
   You should:
   - describe what the animal looks like
   - explain where and how it was found
   - explain why the discovery is interesting.

3. Write a letter to your town mayor arguing against their
   decision to turn your local woodland into a car park.
   You should:
   - explain your reason for writing to them
   - explain the benefits of keeping the woodland
   - write about why the woodland is special to you.

Read the following extract from a story, then answer the question below.

POWERLESS

The lights flickered, then went out. After a few minutes of waiting, our teacher headed down the corridor in search of an explanation for the outage, leaving us in the darkened classroom. At first, our giggles counteracted the sounds of the lashing rain and the grumbling thunderclouds, but as time went on and the lights stayed off, the darkness seemed to grow heavier, and our laughter eventually faded away into silence.

That was three months ago. The lights in our town still haven't come back on.

4. Pretend you are a character in this story. Write a letter to a friend in another
   town about how living without electricity has changed your life.
   You should:
   - describe what your life was like before the power went out
   - explain the ways that your life has changed since the power went out
   - describe how the power going out made you feel.

Summary Questions

Now that you know all the tricks to make your writing interesting, you just need to make sure you use them. Interesting writing isn't something you can do just like that — you have to practise it so it becomes natural. The next time you write an email, a text or even a shopping list, have a go at popping in just a little of the fancy stuff — an inexpensive pumpkin, a lemon as sour as my sister, a bottle of chilli sauce as hot as the sun...

1) For each of the sentences below, change the underlined word to make it more interesting.
   a) The cake was <u>nice</u>.   b) Our holiday was <u>great</u>.   c) That was a <u>rubbish</u> film.

2) List three other verbs that could be used to replace 'to walk'.

3) How often should you aim to use long and clever words?

4) Rewrite the paragraph below to make it more interesting.
   When Olav arrived, we ate some food then we watched a film and then
   we played a game. When Helga arrived, the three of us went to the park
   then we had ice creams and then we went home.

5) Why is it a bad idea to start all your sentences the same way?

6) Is it a good idea to make all of your sentences long and complex? Why / why not?

7) When is it OK to use clichés?
   a) Now and again.
   b) Most of the time.
   c) As frequently as you can.

8) Add adjectives to each of the sentences below to make them more descriptive.
   a) Joseph and Heather walked along the path to the sea.
   b) The car sped through the forest, passing the cottage.
   c) The cow crept into the room, careful not to touch the vase.
   d) There was a noise when the parrot approached the tree.
   e) The man didn't know what was under the table.

9) Which of these are wrong?
   a) You're weirder than me.
   b) She's my bestest friend.
   c) He's more thoughtful, though.
   d) I'm the most funniest.
   e) We're the most charming.
   f) They're much more better.
   g) Pavati is intelligenter than Dani.

Paragraphs

Paragraphs are a pain, but your writing is clearer when you use 'em. You know it makes sense.

Always use Paragraphs

It's not enough to use paragraphs some of the time — you need to use them all the time — in stories, essays, letters... in ANYTHING and EVERYTHING you write.

Paragraphs make things Clear

A paragraph is a group of sentences. These sentences talk about the same thing, or follow on from each other.

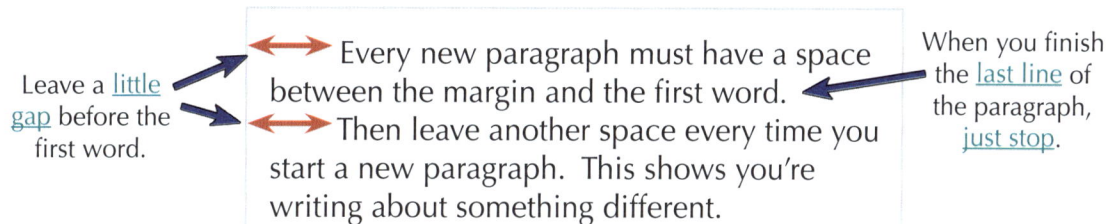

Leave a little gap before the first word.

Every new paragraph must have a space between the margin and the first word. Then leave another space every time you start a new paragraph. This shows you're writing about something different.

When you finish the last line of the paragraph, just stop.

Start a New Paragraph for Each Point in an essay

Paragraphs help make your essay clearer.
A new paragraph shows that you're writing about something new.

Example

This is a new point, so start a new paragraph.

The idea that students shouldn't have to participate in P.E. is controversial. Although some consider P.E. to be less important than traditional academic subjects, it teaches many vital lessons.
In P.E., students learn about the importance of keeping physically healthy. Getting into the habit of being active from a young age can have a positive effect on students' health in later life.

A good paragraph is like a needle — sharp and to the point...

Paragraphs — love 'em (phwoooar) or hate 'em (bleuuurgh), you've got to use 'em. Start a new paragraph every time you start a sentence with a brand new idea, angle or argument.

Using and Linking Paragraphs

You need to know when to start a new paragraph — you can't just guess I'm afraid.

Here's the **Golden Rule** for **Paragraphs**

The Golden Rule — Start a new paragraph every time something changes.

When you talk about a **New Person**

Aida looked at the scene in despair. She couldn't believe that eight soldiers could make such a mess. She sighed and started to pick up the biscuits and crisps.

A friendly face popped round the door. It was Brian. He watched Aida grovelling around in the mess for a second or two before he spoke up.

This paragraph is about Aida.

This paragraph is about Brian.

When **Someone New** speaks

Someone new is speaking, so you need a new paragraph.

"Please don't do that on your own, Aida," said Brian. "Come on, I'll help you clear up."

"Thanks, Brian, you're a star," replied Aida appreciatively. "Where's everyone else? I thought there were five volunteers to clear up."

"They're all dancing over there," he explained.

The same person is speaking here, so you don't need a new paragraph.

A new paragraph for a **New Place**...

The shopping mall was deserted. The guards scratched their heads. Where was everybody?

Outside Bernie's Gourmet Chip Shop in the High Street, it was a rather different story. The crowd was pushing and shoving to get to the door. "Give us battered rat!" they cried. "Give us rat on a stick!"

The story has moved to the chip shop, so this is a new paragraph.

...or for a **Different Time**...

This is talking about a long time afterwards.

At last it was over. The voice called out again, "Are you all right?" I barely had the strength to answer. I was giddy with relief. Soon I would be out of the cave and home.
I don't think about my ordeal that much. When I look back, it seems like something that happened to somebody else.

...or for a **Change** of **Topic**

This is talking about a new topic.

The rugby match last night was extremely dramatic. I still can't believe that Ablington RFC came back to win, given the position they were in at half-time.
The cricket team also played well last night, but were unable to get the victory they worked so hard for. Despite this, there were plenty of positives to take from the match.

Make sure you **Link** your **Paragraphs**

Paragraphs need to flow smoothly from one to the other. This keeps your writing organised. You can use words and phrases at the start of your paragraphs to link them together.

Here are a few examples:

Furthermore...   Therefore...   Firstly...   Another view is...

Secondly...   In addition...   Also...   On the other hand...

... that's one of the main reasons why I'd make a good prefect.
Furthermore, I work very hard, especially in a team...

The word 'furthermore' shows that this paragraph links to the previous one.

... which shows that Justine is a really evil character.
On the other hand, Justine has every reason to hate Sofia...

The phrase 'on the other hand' shows that you're going to look at both sides of the argument.

A herby fish dish — thyme and plaice...

REVISION TASK

Linking your paragraphs together is essential to writing well, so you need to know a variety of linking phrases. Cover this page and jot down all the linking phrases that you can remember, then use a thesaurus or a dictionary to add another 10 words or phrases to the list.

Staying in the Right Tense

Switching tenses is a big no-no. That means you've got to learn to use tenses properly.

Don't change tenses in your writing by Mistake

Once you've picked a tense, you'll usually need to stick to it.
Make sure all the verbs agree with each other.

This is in the past tense.

Another past verb.

> As Andy tried to hide the money, he heard a
> siren in the distance. Suddenly, he sees a light.

This one's wrong — it's in the present tense, but it should
be in the past tense. The correct form of the verb is 'saw'.

Use Past Verbs in Past Writing

1) Be consistent — don't switch tenses accidentally.
   Stay in one tense so it's clear what's going on.

2) If you start writing in the past, you've got to stay in the past.

> The day I finished reading "Jane Eyre" by
> Charlotte Brontë was one of the saddest days
> of my life. I loved the book and had grown
> to love Jane. I knew I would miss her a lot.

All the verbs here are past forms.

If you're writing about the past you should use the past tense.

Be Especially Careful with the Present

You need the present for some essays, but don't mix past and present forms by mistake.

> Even though Alex is injured, Roy felt he has to pick him for the team.

'felt' is past tense, but the rest of the sentence is in the present.

> Even though Alex is injured, Roy feels he has to pick him for the team.

This is how the sentence should be written
— all of the verbs are in the present tense.

Consistency of tenses — a sticky business...

Sticking to the same tense — it sounds so simple. But when you're in a hurry, it's easy to put the wrong one down without thinking. Learn this page and remember your tenses when you write.

Subject-Verb Agreement

Learn these key points on subject-verb agreement — they'll help you gain marks in the exam.

Verbs need to Agree with their Subject

The <u>subject</u> is the person or thing <u>doing</u> the action.

Some <u>verbs</u> change <u>depending</u> on who is <u>doing</u> the action.

<u>Singular</u> subject ⟶ The penguin <u>relaxes</u>.

<u>Plural</u> subject ⟶ The penguins <u>relax</u>.

Watch out for verbs that change in the past tense as well, e.g. 'to be' becomes 'I was', 'you were', and so on.

The verb 'relax' changes to <u>agree</u> with its subject.

Be Careful with Long Sentences

In <u>long sentences</u>, the <u>verb</u> and the <u>subject</u> can get <u>separated</u> — make sure they still <u>agree</u>.

Animals that are raised in captivity, such as the giraffe, is unlikely to survive once they are released back into the wild.

This sentence doesn't work because the verb isn't right — you can't say "<u>animals is</u> unlikely to survive".

It should be "<u>are</u>".

Make sure you can make Common Verbs agree

People often use the wrong forms of '<u>to be</u>' and '<u>to have</u>'.
Make sure you learn the <u>correct forms</u>.

to be		
I am	you are	he/she/it is
we are	they are	

to have		
I have	you have	he/she/it has
we have	they have	

A great page — I think you'll agree...

There are loads of weird <u>verb forms</u> out there that you just have to <u>learn</u>. We've mainly covered the <u>present</u> tense here, but don't forget — a lot of verbs have irregular <u>past</u> tense forms too.

Summary Questions

Well, here we are at the end of another section already, and what d'you know, it's time for a set of Summary Questions. Remember, the point of these little jokers is to make sure that you've learnt something from the last five pages. Go through them, and don't go peeking at the next section until you've got them all right. Ooh, I can be tough when I want to be...

1) What is a paragraph? ☑

2) What should you do at the start of a new paragraph? ☑

3) What effect do paragraphs have on your writing? ☑

4) What is the golden rule for starting a new paragraph? ☑

5) Which of these are moments when you should start a new paragraph?
   a) When the same person is speaking
   b) When you are writing about a new person
   c) When you are writing about a new place
   d) When you are writing about the same person
   e) When a new person is speaking
   f) When you are writing about a different time ☑

6) The following piece of writing is really confusing.
   Turn it into a nice clear bit of writing by re-writing it with three proper paragraphs:

   The biggest challenge facing junior league football today is the sheer number of red and yellow cards issued by referees. There is no doubt that standards of discipline have fallen sharply. This season, 185 yellow cards and 44 red cards have already been issued, with four players facing a four-match ban. Ten years ago, only 53 yellow cards were shown across the whole season, and only eight players were sent off by referees. Players were much better behaved and did not dare to argue with referees. Santiago Perez, Chairman of the UK Federation of Under-16 Football Clubs, said last week that the current situation is "reaching crisis point". Some, like Julian Fortescue of Edenhall School, disagree. ☐

7) List five words or phrases that can be used to link paragraphs. ☑

8) Rewrite the sentence below so that both of the verbs are in the same tense.
   "Steven forgot his hockey stick so he borrows one from Mr Mantell." ☑

9) "My older brother Jeremy, like a lot of people, love going to the cinema."
   Why is this sentence wrong? ☑

Basic Punctuation

This stuff is as basic as punctuation gets. People still make mistakes, though, so learn this page.

Remember these Simple Sentence rules...

Right, here are two rules to remember:

① Every sentence must start with a capital letter and end with a full stop, question mark or exclamation mark.

② The word 'I', the names of people, places, organisations, days and months, and the titles of books and poems ALL NEED CAPITAL LETTERS.

Here are a couple of examples of the rules in action:

You need a capital letter at the start.   Days of the week have capital letters.

> On Tuesday, my friend went on holiday to Greece.

Greece is a place so it needs a capital letter.   There's a full stop at the end.

Months of the year have capital letters.   The word 'I' should always be a capital.

> In August, I am working at Ace Products with Ben.

Ace Products is an organisation. Hello, capital letters.   Ben is a name so it needs a capital letter.

Questions need Question Marks

If you're writing a question, make sure you use a question mark.

> Boris, can you see Mrs Halstead?

Only use One Exclamation Mark

Only ever use one exclamation mark when you're writing a sentence, even if the homework is ridiculously exciting.

Try not to use too many exclamation marks in your writing. It makes you sound over the top.

One exclamation mark does the job nicely.

> It was absolutely amazing! I couldn't believe I was meeting the new pop sensations, The Chinchillas!!!

This makes your writing look like a barcode — and that's just silly.

Getting this wrong — it's a capital crime...

The stuff on this page is the nuts and bolts of punctuation, so make sure you can do it all in your sleep. It can be easy to make mistakes, so just remember to check your work when you finish writing.

Sentences, Phrases and Clauses

It's important that you get to grips with sentences, phrases and clauses...

Every Sentence makes a Clear Point

Make sure that every sentence you write has a clear point.

The Golden Rule — Every sentence must make sense on its own.

A Sentence has to have a Verb

Every sentence you write has to be about something. It can only be about something happening if it's got a verb. (Remember, verbs are doing and being words.)

This is about him buying the ram — "bought" is the verb.

Barry bought a champion racing ram. For £2.50.

You can't do this. There's no verb, so this isn't a sentence. "It cost £2.50." would be fine because "cost" is a verb.

Use Phrases and Clauses to Improve your Sentences

1) Varying the length of your sentences can make your writing more interesting.

2) You can make simple sentences better by joining phrases and clauses together.

   • A clause is a part of a sentence which has a subject and a verb.
   • A phrase is a part of a sentence which doesn't have a subject, or doesn't have a verb (some phrases might have neither).

3) You can join two clauses together to make a sentence:

This is a clause: 'the ram' is the subject and 'likes' is the verb.

The ram likes films, but Barry prefers books.

This is also a clause: 'Barry' is the subject and 'prefers' is the verb.

'But' is a joining word — sometimes you need them to join clauses.

By the way, a main clause is a clause that makes sense on its own (so a main clause can also be used as a sentence).

The ram likes films.

4) You can also join a clause and a phrase to make a sentence:

This is a clause because it has a subject ('the ram') and a verb ('chews').

The ram chews Barry's furniture or his slippers.

This is a phrase. It doesn't have a verb. Nothing is happening.

Santa — my favourite type of clause...

This sentence structure stuff may seem pretty easy, but make sure you understand the difference between a phrase, a clause and a main clause — you'll need them again later in this section.

Commas

You'll definitely need some commas in your writing, so make sure you know how to use them.

Use **Commas** to **Break Up** sentences

If your sentence has <u>more than one</u> point, a comma keeps the points <u>separate</u>.
Commas keep the items in <u>lists</u> separate, too.

> I asked him to shut up, but he kept on yelling.

The comma keeps these two bits <u>separate</u>.

Commas add **Extra Bits** to sentences

You can use commas to <u>add extra bits</u> of information into your sentences.

You can add bits to the <u>start</u> and <u>end</u> of sentences...

> After the match, we all went to Kathy's house for tea and toast.

...or to the <u>middle</u> of sentences. The commas go around it like <u>little brackets</u>.

> Annie and Ali, who live next door, have built a new shed.

commas

When you start a sentence with words like "<u>Oh</u>", "<u>Right</u>" or "<u>Well</u>", you need a <u>comma</u> to separate it from the rest of the sentence.

> Oh dear, I think you need to lose that hat.

comma

comma

> Well, I suppose you might just get away with it.

Don't stick them in **All Over** the place

You should <u>only</u> put commas in when you want to <u>break</u> a sentence up into <u>two bits</u>, or when you want to stick in a bit of <u>extra</u> information.

> The Mayor, Mrs Taylor, and the Treasurer, Mr Barker, said today, that the community centre would open on the 14th of August.

<u>This</u> comma's <u>wrong</u> — "said today" and "that the community centre..." go together — they're part of the <u>same</u> bit of info.

REVISION TASK

I made a film about punctuation — it's a comma-dy...

It's no good chucking commas around willy-nilly — you <u>need</u> to know the <u>right</u> way to use them. Cover this page, write the two uses of commas and an example sentence for each one.

Colons and Semicolons

Colons and semicolons are the big organisers of the punctuation world.

Use Colons to Introduce a List

This is a <u>colon</u>: ➡ :

If you want to <u>introduce</u> a <u>list</u>, you use a colon.

> This is what you need to go camping: one tent, a gas stove, board games, two saucepans, a kettle and a torch.

<u>Only</u> use a colon to introduce a list if it follows a <u>main clause</u> (see p.80). If this sentence started with "you need", you <u>wouldn't</u> use a colon because that's <u>not</u> a main clause.

A Colon can Introduce an Explanation

Colons are also <u>handy</u> for showing that you're about to <u>explain</u> a point you've just made.

> Mr Hackett was feeling very stupid: he'd forgotten to pack any trousers.

Remember, the <u>first part</u> of the sentence needs to be a <u>main clause</u> — it has to <u>make sense</u> on its <u>own</u>.

colon

The bit <u>after</u> the colon <u>explains</u> what was said before — it explains <u>why</u> Mr Hackett was feeling very stupid.

Use Semicolons to Break Up Lists

<u>Semicolons</u> can help you to organise <u>long lists</u> and make them <u>easier</u> to <u>read</u>. They're <u>particularly</u> handy when you want to <u>organise</u> a list that has <u>other punctuation</u> in it too.

The <u>first part</u> of the sentence is, you guessed it, a main clause.

> Lizi's reasons for not going to school were quite simple: she hated being told where to go and when; the school dinners (which were compulsory) always tasted foul; and the uniform, a bright yellow, was just not her colour.

The semicolons divide the list into <u>sections</u>...

...and then you can divide these up using <u>other</u> punctuation.

Semicolons can Break Up Clauses in a Sentence

You can use semicolons to <u>break</u> up <u>sentences</u>, not just lists. Both parts of the sentence must be <u>related</u>, and both parts must be <u>main clauses</u> — this means each part should make sense <u>on its own</u>.

<u>Both</u> clauses could be sentences <u>on their own</u>...

> Keisha married her childhood friend; her twin brother, Jacob, married his cat.

...and they're <u>equally important</u> points.

Colons and semicolons — not just for texting :) ;) ...

Colons and semicolons will make your writing look <u>dead impressive</u>. Remember — colons <u>introduce</u> things, semicolons <u>break them up</u>. I know which ones I'd rather be friends with...

Apostrophes

Lots of people mess this up — so make sure you know it so well that you'll never forget it.

Use **Apostrophes** to **Show** who **Owns Something**

1) You need to use an apostrophe plus 's' when you're writing about things that <u>belong</u> to people.

Kulvinder's goldfish have all died.

The apostrophe shows that the goldfish belong to Kulvinder.

'Men', 'women' and 'children' follow the same rule.

The women's race was cancelled.

2) There's an <u>important</u> rule for words <u>ending</u> in '<u>s</u>':

James's garden is bigger than mine.

If a <u>single name</u> ends in '<u>s</u>', you <u>still</u> need to add an <u>apostrophe</u> and an '<u>s</u>'...

I washed the players' kit in soy sauce.

...but when it's a <u>group</u> of something ending in '<u>s</u>', add an <u>apostrophe</u>, but <u>no 's</u>'.

You can also use **Apostrophes** to **Shorten** words

When you're <u>shortening</u> a <u>word</u> you need to use an <u>apostrophe</u> to show there are <u>missing letters</u>. These are called <u>contractions</u>. Here are some common examples...

I am — I'm	he is — he's	who is — who's
I would — I'd	we are — we're	we will — we'll
I have — I've	they are — they're	does not — doesn't
it is — it's	cannot — can't	will not — won't

See p.88 for more about when to use '<u>it's</u>' with an apostrophe.

'<u>Can't</u>' and '<u>won't</u>' are a bit <u>different</u> — 'can't' is just a shorter version of '<u>cannot</u>', and '<u>won't</u>' <u>doesn't</u> quite <u>match</u> the missing letters from '<u>will not</u>'.

You can use these for <u>informal</u> writing, but for <u>formal</u> stuff, like <u>essays</u>, you should always use the <u>full version</u>.

REVISION TIP

An award for postmen — a post trophy...

Use apostrophes to show that something <u>belongs</u> to someone or that a word is <u>missing</u> letters. Remember <u>not</u> to use an apostrophe to show that there's more than one of something.

Speech Marks

Speech marks do what their name suggests — they show when someone's speaking.

Speech Marks show when someone is Speaking

Every time someone speaks in a sentence you need to shove some speech marks in there.

> "Don't leave the cage door open," warned Sally.

Speech marks surround everything that Sally said.

> Sally warned him not to leave the cage door open.

Careful — this doesn't need speech marks because no one's actually speaking.

Start with a Capital Letter...

Make sure that the spoken bit always starts with a capital letter, even if it isn't at the beginning of your sentence.

> Harry said, "Don't worry, I won't."

It starts with a capital letter.

...Always end with some form of Punctuation

The spoken bits of your sentences need to end with some kind of punctuation. It's usually either a full stop, a comma or a question mark — but make sure you use the right one, and put it inside the speech marks.

> Ruby said, "I knew you shouldn't have trusted Harry."

The sentence is finished, so you need a full stop.

> "He's useless," she declared.

The speech has finished but the sentence hasn't. You need a comma here, not a full stop.

> "Did we feed the bear before it escaped?" asked Rana.

This speech is a question, so it ends with a question mark.

Careful — you don't carry on with a capital letter.

Speech marks — 10 out of 10 for a good 'un...

Don't EVER forget to put speech marks around something that a person's actually saying. The stuff on punctuation in speech marks is a bit harder, so make sure you learn the rules.

Summary Questions

You have to pay attention to all the little details like full stops and apostrophes. It's no good being vaguely aware of punctuation and hoping for the best — you have to know it back to front and inside out. And the only way to make sure you know it all is to go over these questions until you get every single one right — effortlessly.

1) What's wrong with the following sentence?
I've got tickets to see the raiders play the vikings on saturday. ☐

2) How many exclamation marks should you put at the end of a sentence? ☐

3) What's the Golden Rule of sentences? ☐

4) Re-write this as three proper sentences:
I had to find out where the sound was coming from, as I walked closer I got more and more nervous, I wanted to scream, but nothing came out of my mouth. ☐

5) "Under a palm tree with a cool drink."
Why isn't this a sentence? What's missing from it? ☐

6) Are these proper sentences? If not, write a proper sentence instead:
a) My amazing holiday.   b) The sea was warm.   c) To the beach. ☐

7) What is:
a) a clause?   b) a phrase? ☐

8) Put a comma in the right place to show there are two clear points here:
I tried to warn him but the General sat down firmly on the broken chair. ☐

9) Put commas in the right places to show which is the extra information:
The Masked Mathematician her hair streaming out behind her hurtled towards the long division sum. ☐

10) Should you use a colon or a semicolon in the following situations:
a) To introduce a list?   b) To break up lists?   c) To break up clauses in a sentence? ☐

11) What two things do apostrophes do? ☐

12) Put an apostrophe into each of the words below to create contractions correctly:
a) cant   b) Id   c) dont   d) whos   e) theyre ☐

13) Put speech marks and correct punctuation into this sentence:
There's nothing better than a nice cosy armchair murmured Greta. ☐

14) What's wrong with the following sentence?
Terry said "next week I can show you how the equation was solved" ☐

There/Their/They're and Your/You're

Don't throw away easy marks — learn how to use these commonly confused words correctly.

Learn these Different spellings

'There', 'their' and 'they're' sound the same but they have different spellings and meanings:

1) 'There' refers to places and positions.
2) 'Their' means 'belonging to them'.
3) 'They're' is short for 'they are'.

> There is the dictionary — it's under the table.

> Every reader has their own opinion.

> Sue and Jack were born on the same day. They're having a joint birthday party.

Avoid using 'They're' in the Exam

Try not to use 'they're' in the exam — it's too informal. Make sure you use 'they are' instead.

The first two stanzas include lots of emotional language because they're about the poet's childhood.	The first two stanzas include lots of emotional language because they are about the poet's childhood.

Don't get 'Your' and 'You're' Confused

1) 'Your' means 'belonging to you'.

> Your spelling and grammar are important in the exam.

This shows that the spelling and grammar belong to you.

2) 'You're' is short for 'you are'.

> You're going to have to learn this page if you want to do well.

'You're' is a contraction of "you" and "are".

3) Again, try to avoid using 'you're' in the exam — it's informal. Stick with 'you are'.

There, their, they're — it's nearly over...

People always make mistakes with these words. It's easy to do because they sound the same.
This kind of mistake will lose you marks, though, so it's important to get them learnt now.

Weather/Whether and Affect/Effect

These words are a bit tricky. Make sure you don't get your 'a's and 'e's mixed up in the exam.

'Weather' and 'Whether' have different Meanings

'Weather' and 'whether' sound exactly the same. The way they're spelt is also pretty similar, but their uses and meanings are totally different.

Weather

'Weather' is a noun —
it refers to the climate.

Whether

'Whether'
introduces options.

We're wondering whether you'd like to come sailing with us?

I'm not sure. Let me check whether the weather will be any good or not.

You can usually leave off 'or not' if you want.

'Affect' and 'Effect' crop up all the time

1) 'Affect' is a verb — it's an action which influences something else.

This potion will affect your life choices.

The potion is doing something to your life choices.

2) 'Effect' is a noun — it's the result of an action.

The potion will have an effect on your life choices.

This is talking about the result of taking the potion.

3) You could invent mnemonics to help you remember these spellings, e.g. to remember that Affect is a Verb and Effect is a Noun:

All Vampires Eat Nachos.   or   Ants Vanish Easily Now.

A mnemonic is a phrase that includes a certain pattern of letters to help you remember something.

You say effect, I say affect...

Nope, you can't randomly pick a word to use. 'Affect' and 'effect' are separate words — there's a correct one for each situation. The same goes for 'whether' and 'weather'. Learn which is which.

It's/Its and To/Too/Two

These little words are mightily important, so make sure you don't get them wrong in the exam.

'It's' and 'Its' are easily Confused

1) 'It's' is short for 'it is' or 'it has'.

| It's important to feed your cat. |

'It's' is used instead of 'it is'.

| A dog will fetch sticks until it's had enough. |

Here, 'it's' is used instead of 'it has'.

2) 'Its' means belonging to 'it'.

| The fox hurt its tail and jumped into the air. |

Never use its' — it doesn't mean anything.

3) There's an easy way to check if you've used the right version — replace 'it's' or 'its' with 'it is' or 'it has'. If the sentence makes sense, use 'it's'. If not, use 'its'.

| It is time for lunch now. |

This makes sense, so use 'it's'.

| What happened to it is tail? |

This doesn't work, so use 'its'.

'To', 'Too' and 'Two' mean Different things

'To', 'too' and 'two' have totally different meanings:

1) 'To' can mean 'towards' or it can be part of a verb.

| Eric is going to school. | | I am going to write a brilliant essay. |

2) 'Too' means 'too much' or 'also'.

| Phil ate too much cake. | | Helen baked some scones too. |

3) 'Two' means the number '2'.

| There are only two tortoises at the zoo. |

Is that a to-too train? No, it's an owl — twit two...

REVISION TIP

Get in the habit of checking your work for spelling mistakes every time you answer a practice question. This means you'll know what mistakes to watch out for when you're in the exam.

Where/Were/Wear/We're

These words look similar, but they have different meanings. Make sure you use them correctly.

'Where' is used for Places

The word 'where' is used for places and positions. It can be used as a question word or as part of a sentence.

Don't forget about the silent 'h' in 'where'. Otherwise it'll say 'were'.

> Where are these meant to go?

> Shiver my timbers, we're back where we started.

'Were' and 'Wear' are Verbs

1) 'Were' is the third person plural past form of 'to be'.

> When a team finishes bottom of the league, they are relegated.

> When the team finished bottom of the league, they were relegated.

2) You 'wear' clothes.

> You must wear safety goggles when using chemicals.

'We're' is a Shortened Form

'We're' is a contraction of 'we are'. You should only use 'we're' in informal situations.

A contraction is a shortened form of a word (see p.83). The missing letters are marked by an apostrophe.

> We're very casual and informal, so we're using the shortened form.

> We are extremely posh and formal, so we are using the two words separately. None of these ghastly contractions. Perish the thought!

Study this here, there and every-where/were/wear...

These words are seriously important for the exam — they're easy to get wrong because it only takes one wrong letter or a missed apostrophe to change the meaning of a word.

Two Words

Some words might feel like they belong together, but they should be written as two words...

'A lot' means 'many'

'A lot' is another way of saying 'many'. It is always written as two words.

> Trevor has written a lot of books.

> The first paragraph contains a lot of similes.

'No one' is two words

You should write 'no one' as two words, not one.

You might also see it written with a hyphen — 'no-one'. This is fine too.

> No one has ever been to Neptune.

> Ian thought that no one had applied for the job.

'Thank you' is also two words

'Thank you' needs to be written as two separate words.

> "Thank you," said the polite parrot.

> It's good to say "thank you" to a shopkeeper.

'All ready' and 'Already' mean different things

1) 'All ready' is a phrase which means 'completely prepared'.

> The family is all ready to go on holiday.

> Sara was all ready to take the exam.

2) 'Already' refers to something that has happened before now, or started happening before now.

> I've already bought enough food.

> The sun had already set when Gran woke up.

All ready? All set? All go...

Thank you for getting this far — the section is almost over and you've covered a lot of important spellings. No one is perfect, though, so make sure you've learnt this page properly.

Summary Questions

Ok, so that's the end of the spelling pages. Phew. I am going to have to ask you to complete these questions, though. Go through them now and if there are any that you can't answer, go back and work out what the correct answer should have been. Once you can get all the way through without making any mistakes, you're sorted. You'll be a spelling pro in no time.

1) What's wrong with this sentence? "My parents say their looking for they're lost youth." ☐

2) Why shouldn't you write this sentence in an exam? "The police say they're looking into it." ☐

3) Lisa the Lamb wrote the poem below for her friend.
Rewrite the poem, correcting all of the words that are spelt incorrectly.

Your a ewe like me, you are.
In fact, your my shining star.
Of you're friends I think the most of you
So I'll stick to you're side like glue. ☐

4) Correct this sentence:
"Do you know weather the whether will be nice for the race tomorrow?" ☐

5) What's the difference between 'affect' and 'effect'? Make up a mnemonic to help you remember the difference between the two. ☐

6) My brother asked me to name two occasions when I would use 'its".
Why is this a trick question? ☐

7) How can you check if you've got the right version of 'it's' and 'its'? ☐

8) What is the difference between 'to', 'too' and 'two'? ☐

9) When would you use the word 'where'? ☐

10) What's the difference between 'were' and 'wear'? ☐

11) My aunt is terribly formal — she talks like she's reading an exam script.
Do you think she would be more likely to use 'we're' or 'we are'? ☐

12) Correct the mistake in the sentence below:
"My friend and I love the cinema — we go there alot." ☐

13) Which of the words in the brackets should be used to complete the sentence?
"Samantha drove to the hotel and she was (all ready / already) there when I arrived." ☐

Answers

Section Two — Reading: The Basics

Page 4 — Revision Task

E.g. In the play *Blood Brothers* by Willy Russell, the character of Mrs Johnstone is described as looking older than she actually is. This creates sympathy for her character, as it suggests that she has had a difficult life. Mrs Johnstone also says that if she gives birth at the weekend, she "won't even need to take one day off", which shows how hard she works to support her children. This encourages the audience to feel respect for her.

Page 7 — Revision Task

E.g. The brook is said to "murmur under moon and stars", which creates a peaceful atmosphere. This contrasts with when the brook is said to "bicker down a valley", which gives the impression that the brook sometimes flows more quickly and loudly. Tennyson uses words relating to speech, such as "murmur" and "bicker", to emphasise how alive the brook seems.

Page 12 — Warm-Up Questions

1) It is third-person narration. It uses "He" and "his".

2) to entertain and inform

3) The author is writing about themselves, so they will be giving a one-sided view of events to try and help the reader see things from their perspective.

Pages 14-15 — Practice Questions

1) through his body language.

2) It is raining heavily.

3) Polite

4) E.g. Lady Dalrymple seems to have a high social status — she has her own carriage, and her servant comes into the shop "to announce" her arrival, rather than Lady Dalrymple going in herself.

5) E.g. Anne is an independent person — she declines Captain Wentworth's offer of help, saying she would "prefer" to walk. Anne is also respectful and polite. She says she is "much obliged" to Captain Wentworth for his offer, which shows that she appreciates his attempts to help her.

6) Here are some points you could mention:

• There is "a delay, and a bustle, and a talking" in the shop when Lady Dalrymple arrives. By listing these in quick succession, Austen creates the sense that a lot is happening in the shop.

• Austen describes the people in the shop as a "crowd", which creates the impression that there are lots of people in a small space.

• Austen describes the movements and activities of six different characters in just three sentences, which emphasises how many different people are moving about.

Section Three — Reading: The Details

Page 25 — Warm-Up Questions

1) Any five from:
alliteration, exaggeration (hyperbole), metaphors, similes, personification, onomatopoeia and imagery.

2) a) and d)

3) E.g. 'He disliked the present.'

4) When authors use objects or actions to represent ideas.

5) E.g. To emphasise a particular word.

Page 29 — Practice Questions

1) It snows more heavily during the night.

2) the snow had melted.

3) Here are some things you could mention:

• The snow-fairies are "Whirling fantastic". This creates the impression that they are enjoyable to watch.

• The snow-fairies are "fierce" in fighting for "space supremacy". This suggests that they can move aggressively and dramatically.

• The snow-fairies are described as "seeking peace and quiet". This suggests that they do not enjoy conflict.

Answers

4) Here are some things you could mention:

- By personifying the snowflakes as "Snow-fairies", the poet makes the snow seem more magical.

- The repetition of "falling" suggests that an impressive amount of snow is falling from the sky, which adds to the sense of wonder.

- The snow-fairies "flew" through "misty air", which suggests they have magical powers of flight and fly around mysteriously.

- The snow-fairies disappear "stealthily", which makes them seem mysterious and wondrous.

Page 30 — Practice Questions

1) Here are some things you could mention:

- It is very hot. The sun is said to "beat down, beat down hot and fiery". The repetition of "beat down" emphasises how strong the sun's heat is.

- It is very dry. There is only a "little drop of water" and even this is "sucked up" by the sun.

- It is very still. The writer describes how "Nothing seemed to move", and it is so quiet that the noise of the "small sand-hoppers" can be heard.

2) All your points should use relevant examples and terminology, and comment on the effect of the language techniques used. Your answer should be well-organised and clear with correct spelling, punctuation and grammar.
Here are some things you could mention:

- The writer creates a relaxed setting in the extract. Images of a "deserted" beach and the sea flopping "lazily" establish a peaceful atmosphere.

- Alliteration is used in the phrases "prone on the paddock" and "flung over the fences". The repetition of the soft 'p' and 'f' sounds adds to the relaxed tone.

- The writer personifies the bathing-dresses as "exhausted-looking". She suggests that they're resting, which creates a sense of relaxation. The fact that the dresses are exhausted suggests that the people who were wearing them have gone to relax too.

- The writer uses several long sentences in the extract which create a slow and relaxed pace for the reader.

Section Four — Quoting

Page 37 — Warm-Up Questions

1) E.g. 'Tanya felt very uneasy on the way upstairs to her room. It didn't help that it was so dark.'

2) c)

3) E.g. 'Although the ghost disappears, Tanya's feeling that she "hadn't seen the last" of it implies that it will come back later in the story.'

Pages 39-40 — Practice Questions

1) He uses non-standard English.

2) a) E.g. Dickon has an unusual appearance.

   b) E.g. The animals are curious about Dickon.

   c) E.g. Dickon already knows about Mary even though they have never met before.

   d) E.g. Dickon is welcoming.

3) Your plan should include the main points of your essay and quotations/examples to support your points.
Here are some things you could include in your plan:

- Dickon is friendly — when he greets Mary, "his smile spread all over his face".

- Dickon feels comfortable with Mary — he speaks to her "as if he knew her quite well".

- Dickon is used to being around animals — he says that people have to "move gentle an' speak low" around animals.

- Dickon is captivating — for example, a pheasant is described as "stretching his neck to peep out" and hear the "low little call" of Dickon's pipe.

Answers

Section Five — Writing: The Basics

Page 44 — Revision Task

Here's an example of how you could plan your leaflet:

- Effects on plants/animals — can cause poisoning, spread diseases and destroy natural habitats

- Spoils outdoor areas — litter is an eyesore, can create bad smells and make waterways unclean

- Cost of littering — money spent on cleaning up litter could be spent on other things

- Solutions — educate people about the effects of littering, more severe penalties for people who litter

Page 51 — Warm-Up Questions

1) Signposting is when you use your introduction to clearly set out what you will write about in the rest of your text.

2) Formal letters have a more detached tone, often use complex vocabulary and avoid contractions and exclamation marks. Informal letters sound more natural — they often use contractions, chatty language and exclamation marks.

3) True

Page 52 — Practice Questions

1) Answers need to follow the layout, tone and style expected of an informal letter. Language techniques should be used to express your personal thoughts and feelings. Your answer should be well-organised and clear with correct spelling, punctuation and grammar.
Here are some techniques you could include:

- Chatty language: e.g. I had such a blast while I was on holiday — I really wish that you'd been able to make it. I think you would've loved the caves we found and explored. They were pretty cool.

- Exclamation marks: e.g. You won't believe what we found down there — a fossilised shark's tooth!

2) Your answer should be written in an appropriate narrative style and have a clear structure. The content of your story should show that you've considered the title given in the question. Language techniques should be used to catch the attention of the reader, and your story should use correct spelling, punctuation and grammar, as well as a wide range of vocabulary.

3) Answers need to follow the layout, tone and style expected of a blog post. Language techniques should be used to catch the attention of the reader, and your answer should be well-organised and clear with correct spelling, punctuation and grammar.
Here are some techniques you could include:

- Awareness of audience: e.g. So, you're in Oakley for the weekend and need some things to do? Well look no further: this post will tell you all about the best attractions in town.

- Personal opinion: e.g. There are many fun things to do, but my absolute favourite place is the trampoline park. What could be better than spending a few hours jumping as high as you possibly can?

4) Your answer should be written in an appropriate descriptive style and have a clear structure. Language techniques should be used to catch the attention of the reader, and your writing should use correct spelling, punctuation and grammar, as well as a wide range of vocabulary.
Here are some techniques you could include:

- Descriptive language: e.g. On my perfect beach, the sand shines and shimmers as the rays of the sun reflect off the fine grains.

- Alliteration: e.g. Curious crabs crawl all over the silky sand, searching for shelter.

- Personal response: e.g. I love surfing, so my perfect beach is a surfer's paradise with powerful, impressive waves, glorious weather and a café to relax in at the end of the day.

Answers

5) Answers need to follow the layout, tone and style expected of a formal letter. Language techniques should be used to persuade the reader to change their mind, and your answer should be well-organised and clear with correct spelling, punctuation and grammar.
Here are some techniques you could include:

- Formal language: e.g. I am sure you will agree that the whole school does not deserve to be punished for the disgraceful actions of a small minority.

- List of three: e.g. If we manage to agree on these proposals, our school can become a truly positive, inclusive and productive place to learn.

Section Six — Types of Writing

Page 59 — Revision Task

Answers need to reflect purpose and audience using suitable vocabulary and language techniques. Writing needs to be well-organised and clear with correct spelling, punctuation and grammar.
Here are some techniques you could include:

- Clear introduction: e.g. School uniforms play an undeniably important part in any school. They create a school identity, help to prevent children being bullied for their choice of clothes and remove the social pressure of having to wear different outfits every day.

- Awareness of audience: e.g. I realise that some pupils at this school hate having to wear uniform. However, I believe that our school is a safer and more inclusive place because of our uniforms.

- Facts and statistics: e.g. School uniforms are worn in over 90% of UK schools, and there's a good reason for that.

Page 61 — Warm-Up Questions

1) Using exaggeration to better sell your good points makes your writing more persuasive and helps to convince your audience to see your point of view.

2) factual information.

3) E.g. This is a bad example of writing to advise because the author doesn't suggest any actions to take if you're feeling tired.

4) Emotive language helps to make your speech powerful and moving, which can make your audience more likely to sympathise with your argument.

Page 62 — Practice Questions

1) Answers need to follow the layout, tone and style expected of a formal letter. Language techniques should be used to persuade the reader, and your answer should be well-organised and clear with correct spelling, punctuation and grammar.
Here are some techniques you could include:

- Awareness of audience: e.g. And so, Ms Edwards, I am now going to show you why setting homework on a Friday is not the right thing to do.

- Persuasive language: e.g. Do you not believe that students should be given a mental break from school over the weekend? By giving them homework on Friday, you take away that break and do not allow them to come back to school mentally refreshed on Monday.

- Appeal to the audience: e.g. Having no homework to mark or chase after on a Monday will also help teachers have an easier and less stressful start to the week. This can only help to improve the working relationship between teachers and their classes in the long run, creating a better learning environment for everyone involved.

Answers

2) Answers need to reflect purpose and audience using suitable vocabulary and language techniques. Writing needs to be well-organised and clear with correct spelling, punctuation and grammar.
Here are some techniques you could include:

- Clear introduction: e.g. I will explain how choosing to walk or cycle to school can benefit your health, ease congestion and reduce the risk of accidents.

- Facts: e.g. An increase in walking and cycling to school will help to reduce pollution levels and improve pupils' health.

- Proving the opposition wrong: e.g. Those who prefer to drive their children to school may be concerned about their children being at risk if they walk on their own. However, if more children walk to school, they can walk in a group, providing safety in numbers.

- Impersonal criticisms: e.g. The increase in the number of cars is causing high levels of pollution, which is damaging to our health. Congestion in the roads by the school gates creates a higher risk of children being involved in road accidents.

3) Answers need to reflect purpose and audience using suitable vocabulary and language techniques. Writing needs to be well-organised and clear with correct spelling, punctuation and grammar.
Here are some techniques you could include:

- Facts: e.g. The new sports centre has tennis and squash courts, a gym, a swimming pool and an indoor running track for you to use.

- Clear language: e.g. The sports centre will have an opening event next month. There will be membership discount vouchers for all who attend the event.

- Headings and subheadings: e.g. 'Where is it?', 'What's available inside?'

Section Seven — Using Language Effectively

Page 70 — Warm-Up Questions

1) Any one or more from the following: use commas, full stops or semicolons; change the word order; use alternative connectives.

2) E.g. gasped, grumbled

3) a) blazing sunlight

b) immense mountain

c) bewildering message

4) False

5) Sentences b), c) and e)

6) a) She smiled like a crocodile with a good dentist.

b) It made a sound like two trumpets and a sick donkey.

c) He was as lazy as a sloth sleeping in a tree.

d) It tasted like a biscuit and a cake in one.

7) Version a) because it uses a mix of short and long sentences.

8) c)

Page 71 — Practice Questions

1) Your answer should be written in an appropriate narrative style and have a clear structure. The content of your story should show that you've considered the title given in the question. Language techniques should be used to catch the attention of the reader, and your story should use correct spelling, punctuation and grammar, as well as a wide range of vocabulary.

2) Answers need to follow the layout, tone and style expected of a school newspaper. Language techniques should be used to inform the reader, and your article should be well-organised and clear. It should use correct spelling, punctuation and grammar, as well as a wide range of vocabulary.
Here are some techniques you could include:

- Facts: e.g. The new species of whale is forty metres long.

- Attention-grabbing headline: e.g. Whale I Never: New Species Discovered!

- Engaging language: e.g. Did you think the largest mammal was a blue whale? Well, think again! On a recent expedition, scientists were astounded when an unknown species of whale emerged from the depths, stunning them with its tremendous size.

Answers

3) Answers need to follow the layout, tone and style expected of a formal letter. Language techniques should be used to persuade the reader to change their mind, and your answer should be well-organised and clear with correct spelling, punctuation and grammar.
Here are some techniques you could include:

- Formal language: e.g. I sincerely hope that the argument I put forward in this letter will encourage you to reconsider your plan.

- List of three: e.g. Having a woodland space encourages people to go outside, which helps them to lead happier, healthier and more balanced lives.

4) Answers need to follow the layout, tone and style expected of an informal letter. You should engage with the extract from the story and use descriptive language to make your writing interesting. Your answer should be well-organised and clear with correct spelling, punctuation and grammar. Here are some techniques you could include:

- Chatty language: e.g. I thought living without electricity was going to be an absolute pain, but there are actually loads of good things about it too.

- Exclamation marks: e.g. I can't believe it's been three months since the power went out — it feels much longer than that!

- Descriptive language: e.g. Now that the glaring light from street lamps doesn't restrict my view of the sky, I can see hundreds of stars glittering above me like diamonds every night.

Section Eight — Grammar

Page 75 — Revision Task

E.g. Furthermore, In contrast, Despite this, Meanwhile, Nevertheless, As a result, Consequently, Essentially, Moreover, Finally

Section Nine — Punctuation

Page 81 — Revision Task

- To break up sentences:
e.g. I was running late, so they left without me.

- To add extra information:
e.g. The crocodile, which was huge, looked hungry.

Glossary

adjective	A word that describes a noun, e.g. brown mouse, warm day.
alliteration	Words starting with the same sound, e.g. brilliant brown bear.
anecdote	A short, personal story that is usually interesting or amusing.
apostrophe	Used to show possession, e.g. "Ed's", and missing letters in contractions.
assonance	Words that contain the same vowel sound, e.g. happy black cat.
audience	The person or people reading a text or watching a play.
autobiography	An account of someone's life story written by that person.
biography	An account of someone's life story written by someone else.
characterisation	The way a writer gives information about their characters.
clause	A part of a sentence which has a subject and a verb.
cliché	A figure of speech that has been used a lot.
colon	Used to introduce a list or an explanation.
comma	Separates items in a list, separates extra information and joins clauses.
contraction	The new word made by joining two words together with an apostrophe.
hyperbole	Deliberately exaggerating something to make an unrealistic comparison.
imagery	Descriptive language that creates a picture in the reader's mind.
irony	Saying one thing but meaning another, e.g. "I'm so happy we lost."
metaphor	Describing something by saying that it is something else.
metre	The rhythm and syllable pattern of a poem.
mood	The feel or atmosphere of a text.
onomatopoeia	A word that imitates the sound it represents when you say it, e.g. "buzz".
paragraph	A group of sentences that are all about the same thing.

P.E.E.	Point, Example, Explanation — a good way to answer reading questions.
personification	Describing something as if it were a person.
perspective	Who is telling a story.
phrase	A part of a sentence which doesn't have a subject and/or a verb.
plot	The events that happen in a story or play.
purpose	The reason for writing a text.
rhyming couplet	A pair of rhyming lines that are next to each other.
rhythm	A pattern of sounds created by arranging stressed and unstressed syllables.
semicolon	Used to separate lists of longer things and join sentences.
setting	Where a story or play takes place.
simile	Describing something by saying that it is like something else.
slang	Informal language which often sounds like natural speech.
speech marks	Used to show direct speech. They're also called inverted commas.
stage direction	An instruction in a play which tells an actor how to speak, move or act.
stanza	A group of lines in a poem, also known as a verse.
syllable	A unit of sound in a word, e.g. "jump" has one syllable, "jumping" has two.
symbolism	When something stands for something else, e.g. a lamb symbolises spring.
synonym	A word with the same or a similar meaning to another word, e.g. big and huge.
theme	The deeper meaning of a story, e.g. love, power or greed, etc.

Index